SOME TRUTHS ARE NOT SELF-EVIDENT

SOME TRUTHS ARE NOT SELF-EVIDENT

Howard Zinn in *The Nation*
on Civil Rights, Vietnam
and the "War on Terror"

The Nation.

Introduction by
Frances Fox Piven

Edited by
Richard Kreitner

First printing 2014

ISBN 978-1-940489-17-9 paperback
ISBN 978-1-940489-16-2 e-book

Book design by Omar Rubio
Printed by BookMobile in the United States and
CPi Books Ltd. in the United Kingdom

TABLE OF CONTENTS

HOWARD ZINN IN THE NATION

THE NATION ON HOWARD ZINN

INTRODUCTION

FRANCES FOX PIVEN

T he essays of Howard Zinn collected here remind me sharply of the living man, who was my friend for many decades. Each commentary is written much as he spoke: straight-forward and to the point, invariably penetrating and well-informed, never cluttered with needless complexity or intellectual pretension. What is most distinctive about Zinn's writing is his moral passion and indignation at the corruptions and deceptions and bloodiness of the powerful; his deep empathy for the travails of ordinary people, especially people engaged in struggle. As Eric Foner comments in the final essay here, Zinn was not afraid to speak out about the difference between right and wrong.

Zinn and I became friends when I took a teaching job at Boston University in the early 1970s. I was assigned an office next to his in an out-of-the-way corner of a building on Bay State Road. Our corner was often crowded with undergraduates, many sitting on the floor, waiting for Zinn. It cheered me when he arrived, as soon as he had finished meeting with the students, buoyant and smiling, ready for our milkshake and BLT lunches. He was always eager to talk about the political dramas of the day, the dramas of the big world outside BU, and the endless dramas of BU itself, usually having to do with John Silber, our increasingly maniacal and right-wing president, who wanted to run the university as if he were the ruler of a banana republic.

Readers of this volume are likely familiar with Zinn's opus, *A People's History of the United* States. The essays in this volume are somewhat different. *A People's History* documents the struggles of ordinary Americans for a measure of justice, but it does so at a remove of several decades, and even centuries, from the people and the events it describes. These *Nation* essays remind us that for nearly fifty years Zinn himself was deeply involved in the major twentieth-century struggles for social justice in the United States: the emancipatory movement of African-Americans for civil and political rights and the recurrent movements against America's imperial wars, first in Vietnam and then in Iraq and Afghanistan. These essays are reports and reflections on those struggles, on the courage and imagination of the young people who were the main participants, and on the abuses on the part of the political author-ities, including the Democratic presidents who tried to resist or evade movement demands. And while the issues of today's protest movements are different, there are also remarkable continuities.

The civil rights movement's most urgent demand was the right to vote, which had deep historical meaning for African-Americans, if only because deprivation of that right undergirded the Southern racial caste system. The movement scored remarkable victories with the passage of the Civil Rights Act of 1964 and the Voting Rights Act of 1965. But these kinds of victories are rarely for keeps, and voting rights are again in the cross-hairs. The Supreme Court has struck down part of the Voting Rights Act, and Republican majorities in state legislatures are passing laws to make voter registration and voting more expensive and more difficult in ways that will especially affect black voters. In response, a new protest movement may be emerging among African-Americans. In North Carolina, where one of the most draconian laws was passed, the Moral Monday protesters named voting rights as one of their chief issues.

Zinn was a leading figure in the antiwar protests of the Vietnam era, an experience that informs a number of his essays in *The Nation* and included in this book. His fervent opposition to that war reflected his anguish about his own role as a bombardier in World War II, when the bombs he released from 30,000 feet not only killed German soldiers but also visited mayhem and death on civilian bystanders. His resistance to warmaking was also the result of his reasoned conclusion that wars are simply almost never justified. Whatever the arguments of presidents or dictators about

national interests, the price in the lives and limbs of ordinary people is simply too overwhelming.

By the time *A People's History of the United States* was published, I had left Boston University, but Zinn remained my friend
and we talked frequently. For me, he provided a kind of moral
compass; I always wanted to know what he thought before coming
to my own political conclusions. So I read *A People's History* eager-
ly. As readers probably know, the book tells part of the story of
the American past as a series of spotlights on episodes of popular
struggle. The book remains an astonishing success, selling more
than 2 million copies, used as a text in high school and under-
graduate courses, and spawning a cottage industry of "people's
histories" from below. Not surprisingly, some school boards have
objected. And a number of historians, including historians on the
left, have also been sharply critical. In the main, the complaints
are about what Zinn did not do. He told the story of common
people in struggle, but he failed to tell the story of the elites who
responded to them. Or he failed to explain how elites changed
over the course of American history. Or by spotlighting moments
of struggle, he failed to fill the promise of the title: to give us a
coherent narrative *history*.

I do not share these complaints. I believe that Zinn's ambition
was not to enter the academic lists with a comprehensive history
but to perform a much-needed political and historical service by
shifting our focus from the top of American society to the bottom,

by giving the common people their due in the story of the United States. Still, I had a criticism too. I took for granted that Zinn wanted to inspire his readers, to make them appreciate the activists of the past and to encourage them to join in struggles in our own time to remake the world. But his accounts of historical protests rarely end in victory. Or the victory is tainted by co-optation. Or it is so small as to mock the aspirations of those who fought for it. To inspire, I said, you have to talk about the victories.

I was not asking for bad or distorted history. Rather I thought the history of a densely complicated society is also complicated, and the consequences of popular struggles are therefore complex. But no matter, I was wrong. Howard Zinn's writing, including *A People's History*, and including the essays in *Some Truths Are Not Self-Evident*, do inspire people, not because they promise victories for popular struggles, but because they depict so vividly the purpose and even the joy of a political life.✱

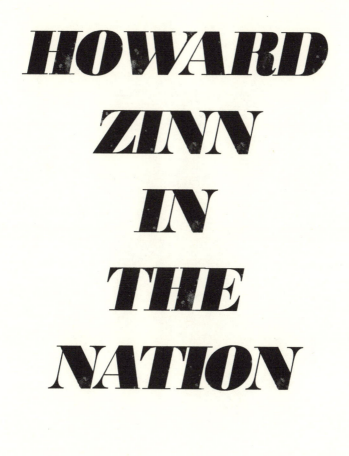

HOWARD ZINN IN THE NATION

FINISHING SCHOOL FOR PICKETS

AUGUST 6, 1960

ne afternoon some weeks ago, with the dogwood on the Spelman College campus newly bloomed and the grass close-cropped and fragrant, an attractive, tawny-skinned girl crossed the lawn to her dormitory to put a notice on the bulletin board. It read: YOUNG LADIES WHO CAN PICKET PLEASE SIGN BELOW.

The notice revealed, in its own quaint language, that within the dramatic revolt of Negro college students in the South today another phenomenon has been developing. This is the upsurge of the young, educated Negro woman against the generations-old advice of her elders: be nice, be well-mannered and ladylike, don't speak loudly, and don't get into trouble. On the campus of the nation's leading college for Negro young women—pious, sedate, encrusted with the traditions of gentility and moderation—these exhortations, for the first time, are being firmly rejected.

Spelman College girls are still "nice," but not enough to keep them from walking up and down, carrying picket signs, in front of two supermarkets in the heart of Atlanta. They are well-mannered, but this is somewhat tempered by a recent declaration that they will use every method short of violence to end segregation. As for staying out of trouble, they were doing fine until this spring, when fourteen of them were arrested and jailed by Atlanta police. The staid New England women missionaries who helped found Spelman College back in the 1880s would probably be distressed at this turn of events, and present-day conservatives in the administration and faculty are rather upset. But respectability is no longer respectable among young Negro women attending college today.

"You can always tell a Spelman girl," alumni and friends of the college have boasted for years. The "Spelman girl" walked gracefully, talked properly, went to church every Sunday, poured tea elegantly and, in general, had all the attributes of the product of a fine finishing school. If intellect and talent and social consciousness happened to develop also, they were, to an alarming extent, by-products.

This is changing. It would be an exaggeration to say, "You can always tell a Spelman girl—she's under arrest." But the statement has a measure of truth. Spelman girls have participated strongly in all of the major actions undertaken by students of the Atlanta University Center[1] in recent months. They have also added a few touches of their own and made white Atlanta, long proud that its nice Negro college girls were staying "in their place," take startled notice. A few weeks ago a Spelman student, riding downtown on the bus, took a seat up front. (This is still a daring maneuver, for in spite of a court decision desegregating the buses, most Negroes stay in the rear.) The bus driver muttered something unpleasant, and a white woman sitting nearby waved her hand and said, "Oh, she's prob'ly goin' downtown to start another one o' them demonstrations."

The reputedly sweet and gentle Spelman girls were causing trouble even before the recent wave of sit-ins cracked the wall of legalism in the structure of desegregation strategy. Three years ago, they aroused the somnolent Georgia Legislature into near-panic by attempting to sit in the white section of the gallery. They were finally shunted into the colored area, but returned for the next legislative session. This time they refused to sit segregated and remained on their feet, in a pioneering show of nonviolent resistance, until ordered out of the chamber.

---

1. The Atlanta University Center is a loose federation of six privately supported Negro colleges in Atlanta: Morehouse College for men, Spelman College for women, Clark College, Morris College, Atlanta University (the graduate school), and the Interdenominational Theological Center. Spelman gets its name from the mother-in-law of John D. Rockefeller. The elder Rockefeller's money put Spelman on its feet. (original footnote)

The massive, twelve-foot stone wall, barbed-wire fence and magnolia trees that encircle the Spelman campus have always formed a kind of chastity belt around the student body, not only confining young women to a semi-monastic life in order to uphold the ruling matriarchs' conception of Christian morality, but "protecting" the students from contact with the cruel outside world of segregation. Inside the domain of the Atlanta University Center, with its interracial faculty, occasional white students and frequent white visitors, there flourished a microcosm of the future, where racial barriers did not exist and one could almost forget this was the Deep South. But this insulation, while protecting the University Center's island of integration, also kept the city of Atlanta for many years from feeling the barbed resentment of Negro students against segregation. Spelman girls, more sheltered than women at the other colleges, were among the first to leave the island and to begin causing little flurries of alarm in the segregated world outside.

Even before bus segregation in the city was declared illegal, some Spelman girls rode up front and withstood the glares and threats of fellow passengers and the abuse of the bus driver. Once, a white man pulled a knife from his pocket and waved it at a Spelman sophomore sitting opposite him in a front seat. She continued to sit there until she came to her stop, and then got off. Spelman students, along with others, showed up in the main Atlanta library in sufficient numbers last year to worry the city administration into a decision to admit Negroes there. The girls spent hours between classes at the county courthouse, urging Negroes to register for voting. They made a survey of the Atlanta airport in connection with a suit to desegregate the airport restaurant, and a Spelman student took the witness stand at the trial to help win the case.

Such activities may bring bewilderment to the conservative matriarchy which has played a dominant role in the college's history, but they are nothing short of infuriating to the officialdom of the State of Georgia, ensconced inside the gold-domed Capitol just a few minutes' drive from the Negro colleges of the Atlanta University Center. Georgia's bespectacled but still near-sighted Governor Vandiver, who resembles a pleasant and studious junior executive until he begins to speak, began his current burst of hysteria when student leaders at the six Negro colleges put their heads together and produced a remarkable document, which was placed as a full-page ad in the Atlanta newspapers on March 9 (and reprinted by *The Nation* on April 2). The document, titled "An Appeal for Human Rights," catalogued Negro grievances with irritating specificity and promised to "use every legal and nonviolent means at our disposal" to end segregation. Vandiver's reaction was immediate: the appeal was "anti-American" and "obviously not written by students." Furthermore, the Governor said: "It did not sound like it was prepared in any Georgia school or college; nor, in fact, did it read like it was written in this country." Actually, a Spelman student had written the first rough draft, and student leaders from the other five colleges collaborated in preparing the finished product.

On the sixth day after publication of the appeal, at 11:30 on a Tuesday morning, several hundred students from the Atlanta University Center staged one of the South's most carefully planned and efficiently executed sit-in demonstrations at ten different eating places, including restaurants in the State Capitol, the County Courthouse and City Hall. Among the demonstrators were several carloads of Spelman students, riding into town that morning without the knowledge of deans or presidents or faculty, to participate in the sit-ins, tangle with the police and end up in prison.

Of the seventy-seven students arrested, fourteen were Spelmanites; and all but one of the fourteen were girls from the Deep South, from places like Bennettsville, South Carolina; Bainbridge, Georgia; Ocala, Florida—the Faulknerian small towns of traditional Negro submissiveness.

The Atlanta *Constitution* and the *Journal* noted the remarkable discipline and orderliness of the demonstration. Perhaps their training came in handy; in prison, Spelman girls were perfect ladies. A Spelman honor student sat behind bars quietly reading C. S. Lewis's *The Screwtape Letters*, while flashbulbs popped around her.

The State of Georgia, however, reacted with a special vindictiveness. To the seventy-seven sit-inners, the Fulton County prosecutor has added the names of the six students who wrote and signed "An Appeal for Human Rights." All eighty-three are facing triple charges of breaching the peace, intimidating restaurant owners and refusing to leave the premises, the penalties for which add up to nine years in prison and $6,000 in fines. The use of "conspiracy" charges to tie all eighty-three students to each of the ten eating places creates a theoretical possibility of ninety-year sentences. Nothing is fantastic in this state.

On May 17, to commemorate the 1954 Supreme Court decision, over a thousand students marched through downtown Atlanta to a mass meeting at the Wheat Street Baptist Church, while a hundred hastily summoned state troopers guarded the Capitol a few blocks away with guns, billy clubs and tear gas. The students were heavily armed with books and songs, and when they were assembled in the church sang, "That Old Negro, He Ain't What He Used to Be!"

What is the source of this new spirit which has angered the state administration and unsettled the old guardians of genteel passivity? There is something fundamental at work which is setting free for the first time the anger pent up in generations of quiet, well-bred Negro college women, not only at Spelman College, but at Fisk, Bennett, Alabama State and other institutions throughout the South. The same warm currents which are loosening the ice-blocks of the *status quo* throughout the world are drifting into the South and mingling with local eddies of discontent. What has been called a global "revolution in expectations" rises also in the hearts and minds of Southern Negroes.

Expanding international contacts are reaching even into small Southern colleges. The arrested Spelman girl from Bennettsville,

South Carolina, spent last year in Geneva studying international relations, and spent the summer in Soviet Russia. The Atlanta student who helped draft the appeal had just returned from a year of studying music in Paris. Last September, two young African women, under the auspices of the militant Tom Mboya, flew in from Kenya to enroll at Spelman. The tame-sounding phrase "cultural exchange" may have revolutionary political implications.

Like many Negro campuses in the South, Spelman is losing its provincial air. This spring, the first white students came—five girls from Midwestern colleges who are the advance guard of a long-term exchange program. In the past few months there has been a sudden burgeoning of contact, both intellectual and social, with students from the half-dozen white colleges in Atlanta. Liberal Southern whites have joined the faculties of Spelman and Morehouse colleges. This growing interracial contact is helping to break down the mixture of awe-suspicion-hostility with which deep-South Negroes generally regard whites. And for Spelman, unexpressed but obvious pressure to adopt the manners and courtesies of white middle-class society breaks down as Spelman girls get a close look at how whites really behave.

The new Spelman girl is having an effect on faculty and administrators. Many who were distressed and critical when they first learned their sweet young things were sitting behind bars, later joined in the applause of the Negro community and the nation at large. Spelman's president, Albert Manley, who inherited the traditions of conservatism and moderation when he took the helm seven years ago, has responded with cautious but increasing encouragement to the boldness of his young women. At the college commencement exercises this year, Manley startled the audience by departing from the printed program and the parade of parting platitudes with a vigorous statement of congratulations to the senior class for breaking the "docile generation" label with its sit-ins, demonstrations and picketing.

Four years ago, a girl in my Western Civilization course spoke candidly and bitterly about her situation and that of her classmates. "When I was little," she said, "my mother told me: remember, you've got two strikes against you—you're colored, and you're a woman; one more strike and you're out—so be careful." The student continued: "That's the trouble with all these Spelman girls. They're careful. They hardly utter a peep. They do everything right, and obey the rules, and they'll be fine ladies some day. But I don't want to be that kind of a lady. I'm leaving at the end of the semester and going back up North."

I don't know where that student is today. She would have graduated with this class on Commencement Day, with students who marched and picketed and sat-in and were arrested, and will soon come up for trial. I wish she had stayed to see. ✳

KENNEDY:
THE RELUCTANT EMANCIPATOR

DECEMBER 1, 1962

The dispatch of federal troops to Oxford, Mississippi, tends to obscure the true cautiousness of John F. Kennedy in the movement for Negro rights. Oxford diverted attention from Albany, Georgia. In the former, the national government moved boldly and with overwhelming force. In the latter, which twice this past year has been the scene of Negro demonstrations, mass arrests and official violence, the federal government showed cautiousness to the point of timidity. The two situations, occurring in comparable Black Belt areas, point up the ambiguous, uncomfortable role of the Administration in civil rights. Oxford is fresh in the memory today and has been the object of an international uproar.

Albany, now in the backwash of national attention, deserves to be brought forward for a good look.

I had the benefit of two such looks: last December, when that Black Belt city erupted with racial demonstrations for the first time in a long history going back to slavery days; and again, last summer, when trouble burst out once more. Both times, the Southern Regional Council, which studies race matters throughout the South from its headquarters in Atlanta, had asked me to investigate and report. What I saw convinced me that the national government has an undeserved reputation, both among Southern opponents, and Northern supporters, as a vigorous combatant for Negro rights.

To be fair, this much should be said at the outset in behalf of the Administration: fundamentally, it is behaving no differently from any of its predecessors. We have always lived in a white society, where even liberalism is tinged with whiteness. I am measuring the actions of the Kennedys not against past performances, but against the needs of our time. My object is not to denounce, but to clarify. It is important for American citizens to know exactly how far they can depend on the national government, and how much remains for them to do. In the field of racial equality, this government simply cannot be depended upon for vigorous initiatives. It will, however, respond to popular indignation and pressure. When I say that it often responds slowly and reluctantly, my intention is not to vilify John F. Kennedy, but to light a candle under the rest of us.

The Kennedy Administration has set limits, never publicized

but nevertheless implicit in its actions, to its own power in the field of desegregation. It will act to keep law and order in cases of extreme and admitted defiance of federal authority, as in Oxford. But it will not act against violation of federal law in other cases—in Albany, Georgia, for instance—where the circumstances are less stark.

There is a rough analogy between Lincoln's insistence (in that famous letter to Horace Greeley) that he was more concerned with *union* than with slavery, and Kennedy's unspoken but obvious preoccupation with *law and order* above either desegregation or the right of free assembly. This explains why the Justice Department, while over a period of nine months 1,000 Negroes were being jailed in Albany for peaceful demonstrations against racial discrimination, gave tacit support to the chief of police for maintaining "law and order." Only after eight months of pressure and complaint did it enter the picture as "friend of the court" in a defensive suit. But it never took the initiative in behalf of Albany Negroes.

The analogy with Lincoln is only a rough one because even the "law and order" principle is applied by Kennedy rather narrowly, with shadowy situations interpreted against the Negro rather than for him. In the case of Ole Miss, the law was unquestionably clear and the imminence of disorder equally clear. But in Albany, there was legal doubt. True, there was an Interstate Commerce Commission ruling and explicit court decisions calling for desegregation of the bus and train terminals. But did not the chief of police say on three successive occasions, when arresting young people who had used the white section of the terminal, that it was not a patter of race, but of keeping "order"? A forthright national government might have dismissed this argument as easily as it did [Mississippi Governor Ross] Barnett's contention that race was not the basic reason for barring James Meredith from Ole Miss. But the Kennedy Administration chose not to challenge Albany's Chief [Laurie] Pritchett.

And when, last December, more than 700 Negro men, women and children were packed into jails in the Albany area for protesting segregation by marching through downtown streets and holding prayer meetings in front of City Hall, the government might have gone to court, on the basis of the First Amendment, to defend the right of free assembly. It might be contended, however, that with Negroes in jail, Albany had more "order." Also, constitutional lawyers disagree over the right of the government to take the initiative in enforcing the First Amendment. The Kennedy Administration has talked of the New Frontier, but perhaps this frontier does not extend into the South or into the field of constitutional law.

Albany is a quiet commercial town in southwest Georgia surrounded by farm land that, in pre–Civil War days, was slave plantation country. Negroes, once a majority in the community, now make up 40 percent of its population of 56,000. Interestingly enough, like many Southern cities just beginning the process of desegregation, Albany has been free of white mob violence of the kind that made headlines at Oxford, Little Rock and a few other places. When, last December, Negroes marched downtown in large but peaceful groups to sing and pray in front of City Hall, whites stood by and watched with curiosity—resentful, perhaps, but quiet. It was the city and county officials who, by jailing the peaceful demonstrators, repeatedly violated the Fourteenth Amendment, which not only prohibits the application of local law on the basis of color, but also—according to constitutional doctrine accepted since the 1920—bars deprivation by local officials of the rights of free speech, assembly and petition.

The fact that it was local police who violated constitutional doctrine is important because it is against local governments, rather than private persons, that the federal government has the clearest right to act in defense of the rights of citizens.

A shaky truce ended the December demonstrations, which had been provoked by arrests at the train terminal, but were rooted, of course, in the total segregation and white domination that make Albany, Georgia, such a hard place for Negroes to live in. By January, the truce began to fall apart. That month, an 18-year-old Negro girl named Ola Mae Quarterman sat in the front seat of an Albany bus, refused to move on the command of the driver, was arrested by a policeman and convicted in city court for using "obscene" language. The driver testified that she had told him, "I paid my damn twenty cents, and I can sit where I want." Subsequently Miss Quarterman told a federal court, to which her case had gone on appeal, that she had used the word "damn" in relation to her twenty cents, not in relation to the driver. (Anywhere but in the Deep South a judge might have thought it incredible that she should be forced to defend her words by making such a distinction.) The city's counsel insisted her race had nothing to do with her arrest, and in cross-examination asked if it was not true that the cause of her arrest was her "vulgar language." She replied softly, "That's what they said."

There followed several hundred arrests as the city police moved promptly against every Negro who, in any way and under any circumstances, challenged segregation patterns: two young men who sat in the Trailways terminal restaurant; four men picketing a store; thirty youngsters asking service at a lunch counter; twenty-nine people praying in front of City Hall; thirty-two Negroes on the way to City Hall; 150 more on the way to City Hall; seven praying in front of City Hall; ten more, eighteen more, sixteen more, all praying in front of City Hall; fourteen praying at the Carnegie Library—all thrown into jail.

After a thousand arrests, Police Chief Laurie Pritchett emerged into national prominence as some sort of hero. He had kept the peace. Somehow, the standard for American democracy accepted by the Administration became the standard for the nation: the sole criterion was the prevention of violence. The fact that violence had at no time been imminent in the demonstrations was overlooked.

There is a statute in the US Criminal Code, Section 242, going back to 1866, which makes it a crime for a local law-enforcement officer deliberately to subject "any inhabitant of any State...to the deprivation of any rights, privileges, or immunities secured or protected by the Constitution and laws of the United States." Under any reasonable interpretation, this law was broken in Albany at least thirty times from November 1, 1961, when police, for the first time ignored the ICC ruling desegregating the bus terminal, to the middle of August 1962, when three youngsters trying to attend service at a white church were arrested. To select one instance with at least fifty witnesses: a county judge watched quietly from his bench as deputy sheriffs dragged and pushed out of his courtroom five young people—one Negro and four whites—who had taken seats in the "wrong" section (by race). One was a young woman whom a deputy dragged over a row of seats and pushed through a revolving door.

The US Department of Justice maintains an FBI office in Albany. Affidavits have flowed into that FBI office in a steady stream, attesting to violations by local officials of the constitutional rights of Negroes. But nothing was done. As recently as last week, the Rev. Martin Luther King Jr. publicly charged that the FBI agents in Albany have been favoring the segregationists.

The Department of Justice, citing a 1943 case in which the conviction of a Georgia sheriff in the brutal killing of a Negro named Bobby Hall was overturned by a narrow Supreme Court interpretation of Section 242, takes the position that it should prosecute only in *extreme* cases of police brutality. This policy allows transgressors of Negro rights who stop short of premeditated murder to act with reasonable assurance that the federal government will not move.

The few things that the national government *did* do in Albany give a clue to the boundaries it has drawn for itself in the field of civil rights: it went into a frantic day of telephone calls when Martin Luther King Jr. was jailed in Albany; King, of course, is a politically important symbol. President Kennedy, in answer to questions on Albany at two different press conferences, made two statements. In one, he criticized Albany officials for refusing to negotiate with Negroes; in the other; he denounced the burning of Negro churches that had been used for voter-registration activities in the Albany area. The President's plea for negotiation, like his careful speech on the eve of Meredith's registration at Ole Miss, carefully skirted the moral issue of racial equality and stuck to procedural questions: the law, negotiation. The President has still not followed the advice of his own Civil Rights Commission to give "moral leadership" and to use "education and persuasion." His statement on church-burning covered two points on which the Administration is especially sensitive: its antipathy to nationally publicized violence and its careful defense of voting rights (but not other rights) guaranteed by the Constitution. The only federal suit initiated by the Justice Department in the Albany area was in defense of voter-registration activity.

There is a plausible legal argument to the effect that voting rights are protected by specific legislation (the Civil Rights Acts of 1957 and 1960), while the First Amendment rights of free speech, assembly, etc., and the Fourteenth Amendment right to color-blind treatment by local officials, are not. However, a national administration, less timorous than the present one, could find solid legal sanction for the widespread use of injunctions to protect free assembly and to attack legal segregation. In the Debs case of 1895, the Supreme Court supported the issuance of injunctions without specific statutory basis, saying: "Every government has a right to apply to its own courts in matters which the Constitution has entrusted to the care of the national government." This ruling has never been overturned.

A truly bold national administration might do the following: (1) prosecute vigorously, under Sec. 242, violations of Negro rights by local officers; (2) create a corps of special agents—not encumbered, as is the FBI, by intimate relations with local police officers—to prevent, as well as to investigate, violations of constitutional rights; (3) use the power of injunction freely, both to prevent policemen from curtailing the right of assembly and petition and to break down legal enforcement of segregation; (4) tell the South and the nation frankly that racial discrimination is morally wrong as well as illegal, and that the nation intends to wipe it out.

At this moment, because of the limitations that the Administration has imposed upon itself, there is a vast no-man's-land for American Negroes into which they are invited by the Constitution, but where federal authority will not protect them. It was into this no-man's-land that the Negro population of Albany ventured, and found itself deserted. The future may bring one or two more Oxfords, but there are a hundred potential Albanys. Throughout the Deep South, Negroes are on the move towards dangerous territory. And so far, though these men, women and children live in a nation whose power encircles the globe and reaches into space, they are very much on their own. ✳

Harry Moss

INCIDENT IN HATTIESBURG

MAY 18, 1964

T here was one moment of sick humor when the four of us in the FBI office in Hattiesburg, Mississippi, met the interrogating agent who had come in to get the facts from Oscar Chase about his beating the night before in the Hattiesburg city jail. John Pratt, attorney with the National Council of Churches–tall, blond, slender–was impeccably dressed in a dark suit with faint stripes. Robert Lunney, of the Lawyer's Committee on Civil Rights, dark-haired and clean-cut, was attired as befits an attorney with a leading Wall Street firm. I did not quite match their standards because I had left without my coat and tie after hearing of Chase's desperate phone call to SNCC headquarters to get him out of jail, and my pants had lost their press from standing in the rain in front of the county courthouse all the day before; but I was clean-shaven and tidy. Chase, a Yale Law School graduate working with SNCC in Mississippi, sat in a corner, looking exactly as he had a few hours before when I saw him come down the corridor from his cell: his boots were muddy, his corduroy pants badly worn, his blue work shirt splattered with blood, and under it his T-shirt, very bloody. The right side of his face was swollen, and his nose looked as if it was broken. Blood was caked over his eye.

The FBI agent closed the door from his inner office behind him, surveyed the four of us with a quick professional eye, and then said soberly, "Who was it got the beating?"

I mention this not to poke fun at the FBI, which deserves to be treated with the utmost seriousness. After all, the FBI is not responsible—except in the sense that the entire national government is responsible, by default—for prison brutality and police sadism. It is just one of the coldly turning wheels of a federal mechanism into which is geared the frightening power of local policemen over any person in their hands.

Chase had been jailed the day before—Freedom Day in Hattiesburg—when a vote drive by SNCC had brought more than 100

Negroes to the county courthouse to register. On Freedom Day, also, fifty ministers came down from the North to walk the picket line in front of the county courthouse, prepared to be arrested.

It was a day of surprises, because picketing went on all day in the rain with no mass arrests, though the picketers were guarded the whole time by a hostile line of quickly assembled police, deputies and local firemen. These arrived on the scene in military formation, accompanied by loud-speakers droning orders for everyone to clear out of the area or be arrested. Perhaps there were no mass arrests because SNCC had been tirelessly putting people into the streets, until police and politicians got weary of trundling them off to jail; perhaps newly elected Mississippi Governor Paul Johnson wanted to play the race issue cautiously (as his inaugural speech suggested); or perhaps the presence of ministers, TV cameras and newspaper men inhibited the local law men.

At any rate, only two people were arrested on Freedom Day. One was Robert Moses, SNCC's director of operations in Mississippi, who has, in his two years or so in the state, been beaten, shot at, attacked by police dogs and repeatedly jailed—a far cry from his days in Harvard graduate school, though not, perhaps, fundamentally, from his childhood in Harlem. Moses was arrested for failing to move on at a policeman's order, across the street from the courthouse.

The other person arrested that day was Oscar Chase, on the charge of "leaving the scene of an accident." Earlier in the day, while driving one of the ministers' cars to bring Negro registrants to the courthouse, he had bumped a truck slightly, doing no damage. But two policemen took note, and in the afternoon of Freedom Day a police car came by and took Chase off to jail. So Freedom Day passed as a kind of quiet victory, and everyone was commenting on how well things had gone—no one being aware, of course, that at about 8 that evening, in his cell downtown, Oscar Chase was being beaten bloody and unconscious by a fellow prisoner while the police looked on.

No one knew until early the next morning, when Chase phoned SNCC headquarters. I was talking with a young Negro SNCC worker from Greenwood, Mississippi, in a Negro café down the street, when the call came in. We joined the two ministers, one white and one Negro, who were going down with the bond money. The police dogs in their kennels were growling and barking as we entered the jail house.

Bond money was turned over, and in a few minutes Chase came down the corridor, unescorted, not a soul around. A few moments before, the corridor had been full of policemen; it seemed now as if no one wanted to be around to look at him. After Chase said he didn't need immediate medical attention, we called for the police chief. "We want you to look at this man, as he comes out of your jail, chief." The chief looked surprised, even concerned. He turned to Chase; "Tell them, tell them, didn't I take that fellow out of your cell when he was threatening you?" Chase nodded.

The chief had removed one of the three prisoners in the cell early in the evening, when Oscar complained that he was being threatened. But shortly afterward the guards put in another prisoner, of even uglier disposition. He was not as drunk as the man who'd been taken out, but he was in a state of great excitement. He offered first to lick any man in the cell. Chase said later, "He was very upset about the demonstration—wanted to know why the jail wasn't 'full of niggers.'" He had been a paratrooper in World War II, and told

Chase he "would rather kill a nigger-lover than a Nazi or a Jap."

The third man in the cell proceeded to tell the former paratrooper that Chase was an integrationist. Now he began a series of threatening moves. He pushed a cigarette near Chase's face and said he would burn his eyes out. Chase called for the jailer, and asked to be removed from the cell. The jailer made no move to do so. The ex-paratrooper asked the jailer if Chase was "one of them nigger-lovers." The jailer nodded.

What Oscar Chase remembers after that is that the prisoner said something like, "Now I know why I'm in this jail." Then:

> The next thing I can remember was lying on the floor, looking up. I could see the jailer and some other policemen looking at me and grinning. I could also see the other prisoner standing over me, kicking me. I began to get up, was knocked down again, and then heard the door of the cell open. The cops pulled me out and brought me into another cell, where I remained by myself for the rest of the night.... I was still bleeding, a couple of hours after the incident.... Watching from the door of my new cell, I saw the trusty put a pack of cigarettes and some matches under the door of my attacker's cell. Later I heard police come in and let him out. I could hear them laughing.

The FBI dutifully took photographs of Oscar Chase and long, detailed statements. Those experienced in the civil rights activities of the past few years will be astonished if anything comes of that.

The beating of Oscar Chase was not extraordinary. In fact, it was a rather mild example of what has been happening for so long in and out of police stations. White field secretaries for SNCC have been beaten again and again in the Deep South: William Hansen had his jaw broken in a jail cell in Albany, Georgia; Richard Frey was attacked on the street in Greenwood, Mississippi; Ralph Allen was beaten repeatedly in Terrell County, Georgia, and John Chatfield was shot in the same county; Robert Zenner has been beaten too many times to record.

Negroes have been beaten more mercilessly, more often, and with less attention: legs have been broken by policemen, faces smashed to a pulp, clubs used again and again on the heads and bodies of black men, women, children. In towns in Georgia, James Williams had his leg broken by police (Americus); Rev. Samuel Wells was kicked and beaten by police (Albany); Mrs. Slater King, five months pregnant, was punched and kicked by a deputy sheriff (Camilla), and later lost her baby. In Winona, Mississippi, Mrs. Fannie Lou Hamer and Annelle Ponder were beaten by police. Men, women and children were clubbed in Danville, Virginia, by police. In a Clarksdale, Mississippi, police station, a 19-year-old Negro girl was forced to pull off her clothes and was then whipped. The list is endless. The FBI has faithfully recorded it all.

Probably the nation doesn't know. It is very much like the Germans and the death camps. There they are, all around us, but we honestly don't see them. Those Americans who do know don't seem to care. Some express concern, but also a sophisticated resignation. Fresh indignation by the naïve is met with a knowing smile. "Man, where have you *been*?" After all, long before and far outside the civil rights movement people have been beaten by police, in and out of jail houses, in every state of the Union. We do have what is called "due process" in the United States, but in that long gap between the moment when a friendless individual encounters an armed policeman to the moment when the normal processes of judicial procedure begin to work, the Constitution too often does not exist.

Something needs to be done, at last, about police and jail-house brutality in this country. Perhaps, to start in a moderate and respectable way, some foundation should subsidize a national investigation, supervised by a panel of distinguished jurists, political scientists and churchmen. But even before that, the President and the Attorney General should be pressed to think and to act on the problem.

We need to stop citing the delicate balance between state and nation in our federal system as an excuse for police tyranny; particularly we need to do so in the South. The truth is that we have not been observing the constitutional requirements of that balance. When the Fourteenth Amendment was passed, a hundred years ago, it made explicit what was implied by the loss of half a million lives in the Civil War—that henceforth state and local governments could not deal with their inhabitants unrestrained by national power. For a hundred years, it has been national law that state and local officials must not discriminate on the ground of color; forty years ago, the Supreme Court began (in the *Gitlow* case of 1925) to rule that, beyond race, the same restrictions on the states derive from the other guarantees of the Bill of Rights. And statutes going back to 1866 prohibit willful deprivation of a person's constitutional rights by local officials.

In other words, the legislative basis for national protection of citizens against local tyranny has existed for a century. The judicial sanction for federal intervention has been in effect for decades, and the Supreme Court has several times made very clear that the President can take any action he deems necessary to enforce the laws of the land. What has been missing—*and it is a void no civil rights legislation can fill*—is the blunt assertion of Executive power, by an interposition of national force between local police and individual citizens. Ever since the North-South deal of 1877 which put an end to any meaningful reconstruction, political interest, caution and the absence of any compelling necessity have combined to leave the Fourteenth Amendment unenforced by the Executive.

What is required now is the establishment of a nationwide system of federal defenders, specially trained, dedicated to civil rights, and armed. These special agents would have at their call civil rights attorneys, prepared to use the federal courts and the injunctive process in much bolder ways than the Justice Department has been willing to adopt thus far. They would be stationed in offices all over the South, but also in the North. With the full power of the national government behind them, they would, in many cases, be able to *persuade* local officials to behave. But they would have the authority—already granted to the FBI, but, curiously, never used in civil rights cases—to make immediate arrests when faced with violation of federal law.

Policemen, deputy sheriffs and other local officials must know that they will *immediately* be locked up in a federal penitentiary if they act against citizens in violation of federal law. *Habeas corpus* and due process will be accorded them, but they will face what thousands of innocent people have endured up to now: the burden of raising bail money, of physically getting out of jail, of waiting for slow judicial processes to take effect. The choice is bitterly clear: either we put up with the jailing and beating of thousands of Negroes and whites who have done nothing but ask for rights asserted in our Constitution, or we put into jail—without brutality—enough local policemen and state officials to make clear what the federal system really is. It is not a matter for discussion in Congress, it is a matter for action by the President of the United States.

Federal interposition is needed at three points in the citizen-policeman confrontation: by its mere presence, to act as a preventive; on the spot at the moment of confrontation (up to now, the federal government, given advance notice of danger, has repeatedly refused to send aid); and in the first moments after confrontation, when quick restitution might still be made of an individual's rights. That one phone call arrested people are often permitted might be made on a "hot line" connecting every local police station with the regional federal defenders' office.

There is genuine misgiving in liberal circles about the creation of such a federal power. But that fear is a throwback to the pre-New Deal failure to recognize that the absence of central power may simply make the citizen a victim of greater local or private tyranny. The storm of economic crisis in the 1930s blew out of sight our Jeffersonian caution in regard to federal power in economic activity. The nation learned that stronger central authority does not *necessarily* diminish individual freedom; it is required only that such authority be specifically confined to designated fields of action.

Our next big psychological and political hurdle is the idea that it is possible—in fact, necessary—to assert national strength on the local level for the protection of the constitutional liberties of citizens. How much more sacrifice will we require from Negroes and whites, bloodying themselves against the wall of police statism, before the nation is moved to act? ✱

THE WOBBLY SPIRIT

APRIL 5, 1965

Review of **Rebel Voices:**
An IWW Anthology, edited by **Joyce L. Kornbluh**

o we see small signs these days—Selma, Berkeley, and who knows where tomorrow—of the Wobbly spirit, still alive? There is a stirring among the young, and talk of a "new radicalism." The timing could hardly be better then, for the publication of *Rebel Voices*.

This is a large, handsome, blazing-red book in which Joyce Kornbluh has assembled a treasury of articles, songs, poems, cartoons and photographs, from the Labadie Collection of IWW documents at the University of Michigan. Those who at some point in their lives have been excited by the story of the Wobblies, and wished it might somehow be kept alive for the new generation, will be grateful to Mrs. Kornbluh for her work.

She introduces the collection with a description of a Chicago meeting hall one June morning in 1905, when the 38-year-old former cowboy and miner, "Big Bill" Haywood, walked to the front, picked up a piece of loose board, hammered on the table for silence, and called out

> Fellow Workers. This is the Continental Congress
> of the Working Class. We are here to confederate the
> workers of this country into a working-class movement
> in possession of the economic powers, the means of life,
> in control of the machinery of production and distribu-
> tion without regard to capitalist masters.

On the speakers' platform with Haywood were two of the great figures of American radicalism: white-haired Mother Jones, the 75-year-old organizer for the United Mine Workers of America, and Eugene Debs, leader of the Socialist Party. Also at the meeting was the sharp-tongued polemicist of the Socialist Labor Party, Daniel DeLeon; the renegade Catholic priest, black-bearded Father Hagerty; and Lucy Parsons, widow of the Haymarket Affair martyr Albert Parsons. That day, the Industrial Workers of the World was formed, and for the next decade (until it was crushed in the repression of the war to make the world safe for democracy) gave the nation its first close look at a revolutionary movement.

In those years, the permanent characteristics of the United

States in the twentieth century were being hardened. There was the growing power of giant corporations (United States Steel had been formed in 1901). A minority of the nation's workers were organized into an exclusive trade union with conservative leadership (the AF of L, under Samuel Gompers, had almost 2 million members). And this era saw the inauguration of benign governmental regulation of business, supported by a new consensus of businessmen, Presidents, and reformers, which traditional historians have called "the Progressive Era," but which Gabriel Kolko (in his book *The Triumph of Conservatism*) terms "political capitalism." In retrospect, the IWW appears to have been a desperate attempt to disrupt this structure before its rivets turned cold.

The IWW played for keeps. Where the AF of L called for "a fair day's wage for a fair day's work," the Wobblies wrote, in the preamble to their constitution.

> The working class and the employing class have nothing in common. There can be no peace so long as hunger and want are found among millions of working people and the few, who make up the employing class, have all the good things of life. Between these two classes, a struggle must go on until the workers of the world organize as a class, take possession of the earth and the machinery of production, and abolish the wage system.

Against the craft union concept (what they called "The American Separation of Labor") the IWW set as their goal "One Big

Union," and in each industry organized the skilled and unskilled, foreign-born and native Americans, Negroes and whites, women and men. They were fiercely militant, opposed to contracts with employers, unyielding in retaining the right to strike at all times. They were suspicious of politics for, as Father Hagerty put it, "Dropping pieces of paper into a hole in a box never did achieve emancipation of the working class." The abolition of capitalism would come, they believed, through a series of general strikes, after which workers would run the industries themselves. "By organizing industrially we are forming the structure of the new society within the shell of the old."

The IWW never gained a mass membership as did the AF of L. At its peak, it probably had 60,000 members: miners, lumberjacks, construction workers and migratory farm hands, with pockets of influence among steel and textile workers. But it shook up the nation as had no other organization of its time.

The Wobblies engaged in dozens of "free-speech fights" in places like Missoula, Montana, and Spokane, Washington, to establish their right to speak on street corners to working people. *Rebel Voices* contains some of the eyewitness reports that came out of those campaigns. In Spokane, arrested one by one for mounting a soapbox, IWW men kept pouring into town, until 600 of them were crowded into the jails, and finally the city officials, after several deaths from brutal treatment in prison, gave in to the demand for free speech and assembly.

In 1912 and 1913, the strikes organized by the IWW reached a crescendo: lumbermen in Aberdeen, Washington, streetcar workers in Portland, Oregon, dock workers in San Pedro, California. The high point of IWW organizing activity, and its greatest victory, came in the 1912 strike of textile workers in Lawrence, Massachusetts. *Rebel Voices* records the account of a strike meeting by journalist Ray Stannard Baker.

> It is the first strike I ever saw which sang. I shall not soon forget the curious lift, the strange sudden foe of the mingled nationalities at the strike meetings when they broke into the universal language of song.

The Lawrence textile strike lasted ten weeks, involved 25,000 men, women and children, and was watched with mounting tension by the entire nation. Paul Brissenden, in his classic history of the IWW, wrote, "Lawrence was not an ordinary strike. It was a social revolution." The section of *Rebel Voices* dealing with Lawrence is one of its best. There are the cartoons (a giant policeman raising a club over huddled women and children), the photographs (a portrait of poet Arturo Giovanitti, IWW organizer in Lawrence), and page after page of personal recollection. A woman observer testified about what happened at the railroad station, where 150 strikers' children were preparing to leave to stay with families in Philadelphia who had promised them shelter and food for the duration of the strike.

When the time came to depart, the children, arranged
in a long line, two by two...were about to make their way to
the train when the police...closed in on us with their clubs,
beating right and left.... The others and the children were
thus hurled in a mass and bodily dragged to a military truck
and even then clubbed.

There is the account of the strike by a 15-year-old textile
worker in Lawrence, named Fred Beal:

Two Italian spinners came to me with a long white
paper: *The Following People Working in the Spinning Room
Will Go on Strike Friday, January 12, If Wages Are Cut.*
Queenie read it over my shoulder. "Don't sign it, Lob-
ster," she cautioned. "Those wops'll get you in trouble".... But I signed it. So did Gyp and Lefty Louze.

There is the testimony before the Congressional committee
investigating the Lawrence strike, by teenager Camella Teoli.

Well, I used to go to school, and then a man came up
to my house and asked my father why I didn't go to work,
so my father says I don't know whether she is 13 or 14
years old. So the man says you give me $4 and I will make
the papers come from the old country saying you are 14.
So my father gave him the $4 and in one month came the
papers that I was 14. I went to work.

A parade of fascinating figures and historic events marches
through the pages of *Rebel Voices*: the young, dark-haired, Irish
IWW organizer in Lawrence, Elizabeth Gurley Flynn, the pag-

eant put on by John Reed at Madison Square Garden for the Paterson textile strikers of 1913, the songs of Joe Hill, the story of his death, and his last cry, "Don't mourn. Organize." There are the lumberjacks and miners and harvest stiffs. Finally, there are the attacks on the IWW by the government after the nation went to war in 1917.

In 1914, the IWW had declared: "We as members of the industrial army will refuse to fight for any purpose except the realization of industrial freedom." A Wobbly orator said: "In the broad sense, there is no such thing as a foreigner. We are all native-born members of this planet. We ought to base in the place of national patriotism, a broader concept—that of international solidarity." The IWW refused to call off strikes because the nation was at war, and a Tulsa, Oklahoma, newspaper wrote:

> The first step in the whipping of Germany is to strangle the IWW's. Kill them, just as you would kill any other kind of a snake…. It is no time to waste money on trials. All that is necessary is the evidence and a firing squad.

The year 1918 brought mass arrests and mass trials of IWW members charged with interfering with the war effort in various ways. Judge Kenesaw Mountain Landis tried a hundred Wobblies in Chicago, and John Reed wrote: "Small on the huge bench sits a wasted man with untidy white hair, an emaciated face in which two burning eyes are set like jewels, parchment skin split by a crack for a mouth; the face of Andrew Jackson three years dead."

The Wobblies went to prison. Big Bill Haywood jumped bail and sailed to Russia, where he died in 1928. After the war was over, the IWW was not the same. A photo in *Rebel Voices* speaks eloquently: it shows the shambles made of IWW headquarters in New York City, after a raid by federal agents in 1919.

Today, the Wobblies live, not so much in the embers of that once fiery organization, but in the people whose lives they changed. They live also in that special way in which art and literature keep the past alive—in Mrs. Kornbluh's book, or in the autobiographies of Bill Haywood, Mother Jones, Ralph Chaplin, and in Wallace Stegner's novel *The Preacher and the Slave.* But when will some audacious American filmmaker match the Italian production *The Organizer* with a motion picture on the Lawrence textile strike of 1912, or the Ludlow, Colorado, massacre of 1914?

Half a century separates the IWW from the militant wing of the civil rights movement today, but the parallels are striking. One might see a sharp contrast in the attitudes toward violence, yet the popular image of the dynamite-carrying Wobbly was overdrawn. The IWW emphasis was on self-defense; the Wobblies' big weapons were the withholding of their labor, the power of their voices. Even their "sabotage" meant mostly slowing down on the job. Consider the other characteristics, however: the plunging into areas of maximum danger; the impatience with compromises and gradualist solutions; the deep suspicion of politics (even in the midst of so imaginative a use of politics as the Freedom Democratic Party); the emphasis on direct, militant, mass action; the establishment of pieces of the new world within the old (the Freedom Schools, etc.); the migrant, shabby existence of the organizer (DeLeon reprimanded the Wobblies for their "bummery," their overalls and red neckerchiefs); the songs and humor; the dream of a new brotherhood.

Somehow, time and circumstance (or is it a feeling of security?) make the Wobblies and the Molly Maguires more palatable today to the country at large. Would those who think romantically of them now have befriended them in the days when they were hated and hunted? It does not hurt to suggest that historical perspective often shines a kindly light on those who disregard some of the proprieties of respectable liberalism in their passionate sweep toward justice. *Rebel Voices* provides such a reminder. ✳

THE SOUTH REVISITED

SEPTEMBER 20, 1965

This essay appeared in The Nation's 100th anniversary issue, and was reprinted alongside excerpts from John Richard Dennett's "The South As It Is," which was published regularly in the magazine during the first year of its existence. Dennett's collected reports are a chillingly modern-feeling account of the South just after the Civil War—he interviewed former slaves and former slaveholders, agents of the Freedmen's Bureau and decommisioned Confedeerate soldiers—and an indispensable read for anyone interested in the history of American race relations.

LYNCHBURG, VIRGINIA. On the Piedmont plane from Washington to Lynchburg at dusk, a plump-faced man in a business suit began a conversation, his accent soft-Southern:

"You going to Lynchburg? So am I. I'm in the pharmaceutical business. Just come from Baltimore, trying to find me a salesman there…. Understanding people is the main thing in selling…. It's like this whole business now with the nigra. Why naturally the nigra's going to demand his rights so long as he's oppressed. And naturally the white man's going to oppress him so long as he can get away with it…. I don't know what your religion is, but this is what I like about Christianity—it preaches moderation.

"Now look, I can tell a nigra's voice any day of the week. I was brought up on a farm outside Greenville, South Carolina, and I played with nigra boys, wrestled with them, fished with them. I can tell their talk anywhere, through a wall, through a curtain, on the telephone, *anywhere*. Well, in Baltimore, this fellow calls me up for an appointment. Very nice, intelligent, credentials first-rate, I couldn't tell a thing from his voice. We made an appointment, he came to the hotel, walked up to me in the lobby. A good-looking nigra, neat, pleasant. We shook hands and talked. I told him I'd let him know later about my decision. Would our company hire a nigra? I don't know. *I* would. The world's coming in on the South."

On a hill south of Lynchburg, an old Negro man, short and thin, in a blue Air Force jacket too big for him, stood outside his wooden cabin and talked, looking out on the road most of the time and only occasionally a quick glance at me. Rain came suddenly and drenched us, and we went up on his porch. A little Negro girl peered through the window at us, disappeared, then came back and looked some more.

"No, this is my son's jacket. I got a pension from the *first* war. My wife works in a dry cleaning place in town, and my son's in the laundry. He's a washer, been there a long time. They throws the clothes in and he washes them. Got two other sons, they works in a foundry in town, makes good money, maybe a hundred dollars a week. Then they start taking off from that and it's not that much.

"Farmin's poor here. I just got two acres. Used to grow tobacco. Now they won't let you grow but an acre. Grow two rows more and they come along and pull it up. They gives you lime to keep the soil good, but all they let you grow is grass. Used to grow wheat, oats, sell them. No more. Oh, I got a half acre planted now, a little onions, cabbage, peas. Too cold to grow potatoes. Yes, the old folks stay, the young ones go, off here, there, everywhere in the world. They work, make just enough for themselves, can't send nothing back to their daddy. Folks remaining here, they go off during the day to work, in Lynchburg, Bedford, far away as Roanoke—fifty miles each way, every day. Farmin's bad around here."

Farther down the road, two Negro women in a two-room cabin of stone and wood invited me into the living room. One of them, slim, animated, with bright red lipstick and a high-pitched voice, did all the talking, while the other sat nearby, not saying anything but smiling at me, nodding her head in agreement with what the other was saying, occasionally interposing, "That's right, that's right." A boy of 6 sat nearby, silent, listening. The walls had dozens of calendar photos, including one of Jesus and one of President Kennedy, and there were hundreds of little knickknacks all over the room. The bed was covered with clothes to be ironed. Nearby was an old TV set and a damaged piano. "Got the piano last year," the woman said, "but it got to be tuned." She waved her hand at the crowded room. "White folks gave me all these.

"No, we got no running water. We'll be putting in a pump soon though. We carry the water from the well, once, twice a day, heat it on the wood stove in the kitchen. Me, I work for a trained nurse. My boy here was playing in her house with her little boy—they got lots of toys all over the house—and she called me over and said, 'Look how my little boy doesn't know about color—they're just having so much fun together.' Yes, he's going to school next year; we got one school integrated—just a little. One ain't."

She pointed to the other woman. "She works in town for other folks. They calls her on the phone at her sister-in-law down the road. White folks been good to us. My house burned down, everybody got together and built me a new one. Folks around here get along fine. Yes, we had a few sit-ins downtown, five and dime is integrated now. But those people on the march in Alabama. They're silly, just plain silly!

"We do different kinds work around here. According to our education—you know what I mean. They *classify* us, fourth grade, sixth grade, eighth grade. And we get jobs by that…. No, I don't vote. It's no use voting. No, no one here stops me from voting I don't see any point to it. They'll do what they want anyhow. I won't make any difference."

On the road from Lynchburg, a poster signified the South. "Sister Christine—Palm Reader." The highway raced the railroad, close alongside, twenty-five miles to Appomattox. The earth beside the highway was angry red where machines had worked. It was early morning, and two Negro girls piled high with books were squirming, trying to keep them intact while waiting for the school bus. Nearby a tiny white girl with a pleated coat and high, yellow stockings raced across a debris-littered field to climb onto a pile of stones, earth, grass, out of which stuck an uprooted, mutilated tree.

A few miles distant, where a cool wind blew unchecked across an open field, was a green granite plaque reading: "Here on Sunday, April 9, 1865, after four years of heroic struggle in defense of principles believed fundamental to the existence of our government, Lee surrendered 9,000 men, the remnants of an army still unconquered in spirit, to 118,000 men under Grant." An iron gate enclosed nineteen tiny blackened stones, representing eighteen Confederate soldiers and one Union soldier, who had died on the day before the surrender was signed.

JOHN'S ISLAND, SOUTH CAROLINA. Out to John's Island, across a neck of water from Charleston, the road is rutted and muddy. There was a shattered bridge across a creek, little houses widely separated, three boys moving through the woods. Negroes turned from slaves to sharecroppers after the Civil War and some bought pieces of land for themselves. But the sons left, and the old folks couldn't pay the taxes, so white farmers bought them out. "Just me one in this house," an old Negro woman said.

Down the road was the "courthouse" where the magistrate, virtual king of the island, held court in an incredibly tiny white wooden box. In front of an auto graveyard, where even the earth was rusty, a Negro woman lived in an old storage shed. In the front yard, a little girl washed clothes in two basins, while her brother rode his twisted bike crazily through the mud.

Back in the middle of the island, in a glen under huge spreading oaks thick with Spanish moss, a white man and a Negro were unloading bright-colored fertilizer sacks from a truck. They were about to plant 600 acres of beans and cabbage. "No, we're not both farmers," the white man said firmly. "*I* farm. *He's* workin!"

Down the road, near a planted field, with hens puttering all around, a young white girl, thin, pimply-faced, held a healthy-looking baby and walked beside her 7-year-old sister. She talked, at first carefully, then more and more at ease. "This is my daddy's land. He plants peanuts and cabbage. But we're moving to the mainland.

He'll come back just for sowing and harvesting. Can't live here no more. Got no one for this little girl to be friend with." She pointed to a cluster of Negro children playing a hundred feet down the road. "Nothin but nigger kids to play with, and Daddy won't let us play with nigger kids. They sicknin, they ugly, that's why."

Later, on the island, in the house of folklorist Guy Carawan and his wife Candie, I pored over the recorded musings of Negroes living on the island.

"The world is a lot of better now; day is past and gone the people use lamps. This is a lot of change, this electric light. In my time coming up people had jimbo light—you put oil in any kind of bottle, and light 'em for see by. Jimbo light. You must pull the string now, your house light go up.... My mother died and gone when I's a girl. Said, 'I may died and gone, but you going see things fly up in the air!' And it's so. The airplane carrying you across, any which way you want to go."

Another. "Whoopin cough, that's what my baby had. Fiddler crab—some little thing down the creek run back in the hole—well you catch that, you put something else along with that, and you boil em. And once you done boil em, you strain em through a white cloth or a strainer. That'll cure whoopin cough."

Children talking—

Girl: "In Charleston I see a colored girl go with a white boy—people I don't know. People around here say that's a disgrace. I don't say is a disgrace."

Johnny: "See lot of em in New York. Lot."

Girl: "My friend told me that she was in New York. And she go sit down on the step or somethin like that, and she watch the girls and boys—the white boys and the colored girls—go by, and they stand right up in the street, and kiss each other."

Johnny: "If they did that on John's Island, the Mayor would come out. Mayor!"

A young girl: "We go dance at 'gressive Club, and Fields, and Bernard…. We do just dances out now. The Jerk, the Camel Walk, and Shake, and the Twine Time. Some old dance been out, the Twist, the Mocking Bird, and the Dog, the Bird, the Fly, the Swim. The people who sing the record come on the television first, and so they is get the dance from the people."

A woman: "I am a mother of ten head of kids. That's enough. Lost three and raise seven head; lost one and got six head. So God take good care of me…. My daughter Hattie have to work. She got two head of kids…. She housework. She go on in with the husband in the morningtime, and she don't be home 'fore seven cause she have wait on husband till he knock off. You know we have to bum for catch a ride back. I do work. I work on the farm. But now my old man sick. Willis sick and I cannot work, cause I have to take care of him. Some days I don't know how I going to lay my weary head, how we going make it."

MONTGOMERY, ALABAMA. The march from Selma, a little over halfway along, turned into a field a hundred yards off the main highway to Montgomery, deep in Lowndes County ("a bad county") and settled down for the night. The field was pure mud, so deep one's shoes went into it to the ankles, and to pull out after each step was an effort. A chunk of moon shone, the sky was crowded with stars, and yet the field was enveloped in blackness. Two huge tents went up, one for men, one for women, and inside people spread plastic sheets over the mud, unrolled their sleeping bags, lay down, weary.

There were three hundred of them, the "core" of the Long March, mostly black people from Selma, Marion and other little towns in central Alabama, but also young Negroes from the Southern Christian Leadership Conference and the Student Nonviolent Coordinating Committee, and some white people, young and old, from all over the nation. Space under the tents was soon gone, so people sprawled outside along the mired road that cut through the field.

At the edge of the field were gathered the Jeeps and trucks of the US Army, soldiers in full battle dress, called out finally by presidential order after thirty days of murder and violence in Alabama and cries of protest through the country.

Moving through the darkness in and out of sleeping forms on the ground were men with white ragged emblems marked "Security." They carried walkie-talkies, the aerials glinting, and communicated with one another across the encampment. There was a central transmitter in a parked truck. People coming in off the main highway were checked at the end of the mud road by two husky "Security" men, young Episcopalian priests with turned-around collars. One of them

said: "I don't really know who to let in. If he's black I let him through."

Lying down in the darkness near the road, I could hear the hum of the portable generators and an occasional burst of sound on a walkie-talkie. The plastic sheet under me was soaked in mud and slime, but the inside of the sleeping bag was dry. Two hundred feet away, in a great arc around the field, were fires lit by soldiers on guard through the night.

I awoke just before dawn, with a half-moon pushing, flat side first, through the clouds. The soldiers' fires at the perimeter were low now, but still burning. Nearby, the forms of perhaps twenty people wrapped in sleeping bags or blankets. The generator still whirred. Other clusters of sleepers were now visible, beginning to awaken.

A line formed for oatmeal, hardboiled eggs, coffee. Then everyone gathered to resume the march. A Negro girl washed her bare feet, then her sneakers, in a stream alongside the road. Near her was a minister, his black coat streaked with mud. A Negro woman without shoes had her feet wrapped in plastic. Andy Young[2] was calling over the main transmitter to Montgomery: "Get us some shoes; we need forty pairs of shoes, all sizes, for women and kids who been walking barefoot the past twenty-four hours."

An old Negro man took his place beside me for the march. He wore a shirt and tie under his overalls, also an overcoat and a fedora hat, and used a walking stick to help him along. "Yes, I was in Marion the night Jimmy Jackson was shot by the policeman. They got bull-whips and sticks and shotguns, and they jab us with the electric poles."

At exactly 7 AM an army helicopter fluttered overhead and the march began, behind an American flag, down to the main highway and on to Montgomery. The marchers sang: "FreeDOM! Free-DOM! Freedom's Coming and It Won't Be Long!"

It was seventeen miles to the edge of Montgomery, the original straggling line of three hundred thickening by the hour as thou-

2. Young, future congressman and Ambassador to the United Nations, was executive director of the Southern Christian Leadership Conference and a leader of civil rights campaigns in Birmingham, Selma and Atlanta.

sands joined, whites and Negroes who had come from all over the country. There was sunshine most of the way, then three or four bursts of drenching rain. On the porch of a cabin set way back from the road, eight tiny Negro children stood in a line and waved, an old hobby horse in the front yard. A red-faced, portly Irishman, newly-arrived from Dublin, wearing a trench coat, held the hand of a little Negro boy who walked barefoot next to him. A Greyhound bus rode past with Negro kids on the way to school. They leaned out the window, shouting "Freedom!" A one-legged young white man on crutches, a black skullcap over red hair, marched along quickly with the rest. Two Negro boys with milky sun lotion smeared on their faces looked as if they had stepped off the stage in Genet's *The Blacks*. A group of white workingmen along the road watched silently. On the outskirts of Montgomery, students poured out of a Negro high school, lined the streets, waved and sang as the marchers went by. A jet plane zoomed close overhead and everyone stretched arms to the sky, shouting, "FREEDOM! FREEDOM!"

VICKSBURG, MISSISSIPPI. As I paid my bill at a motel just outside of Jackson, Mississippi, an attractive young Negro couple, smartly dressed, came down the stairs and into the lobby. A white man, sunburned, in shirt sleeves, leaned on the desk, staring at the couple. The motel manager said, apologetically. "Mississippi school teachers." The white man said, "Should charge them thirty dollars a day!" The manager was silent.

Somehow, I was back on Highway 80, the same that went from Selma to Montgomery, here running west from Jackson to Vicksburg and the Mississippi River. A dirt road cut off toward the horizon and a Negro man on a wagon pulled by two mules waited for a chance to cross the highway. He was glad to talk a while.

"Oh I got plenty of time. Don't have to be where I'm going until maybe about three. Got cottonseed cakes in the wagon, for the cows to eat. You know, cows will eat cotton too, right off the ground, just cause it's white. Funny how it is, we grows the seed, then buys it back from the mill, dollar and a quarter a hundred pound sack.... No, these ain't mine. Man I work for, he's got over a hundred cattle. His land goes a mile. I don't make enough to talk about. Three dollars a day. I work three days a week sometimes. And I got six children out the house. You come out less than you started."

The highway approaches the Mississippi just south of Vicksburg, the river impressive at that point, wide, slow, misty, the opposite shore dim, the Yazoo River sweeping in from the Northeast. In the bend near the shore were railroad tracks, storage bins, smoke gushing from stacks, and the sound of engines.

In Vicksburg, the county courthouse carried a sign that it was built under Franklin D. Roosevelt and the Public Works Administration. Inside the Registry office, on the counter, were two massive books bound in red leather. One was inscribed: WARREN COUNTY MARRIAGE RECORD — WHITE; the other: WARREN COUNTY MARRIAGE RECORD — COLORED.

Two miles up the river, I turned into the yard of a large feed mill and signed in at the shack of a guard before being allowed to go to the president's office. A distinguished-looking man, with an accent mildly Southern, he was at first wary and unsmiling, but soon became more friendly.

"This is, I guess, the biggest mill in the area. No, I don't own it. It's part of a big Mississippi company that has all sorts of diversified interests: feed mills, grain merchandising, breeder flocks of broilers, hatcheries—maybe 200,000 layers and 60,000 dozen eggs a week—hog operations, meat packing, steel, paper. I guess twenty to twenty-five families control the majority of stock; we are really a Mississippi company, which is rare these days; we've got no major Northern stockholders. Here at this mill we process grains and seed. Yes, we make these cottonseed cakes for cattle feed—we call them 'range cubes.' Strange how history comes back at you; water transport is more important again, because operations are bigger. Grain used to come in sacks, now it comes in bulk, and for that barges are best to send the grain down the Mississippi. Can ship twenty-five times as much in a barge as in a boxcar.

"We in the Chamber of Commerce are trying to move Vicksburg ahead. Nine years ago, when I came here (Kansas City is my home) it was a sleepy town, completely devoted to the past. Tourism was the big thing. You know we have these battlefields all around, monuments and statues. People wanted to leave things as they were.

There's still a lot of old thinking in town, but that's what we're trying to change. This town has a big potential. It's a crossroads.

"Twenty-five percent of my boys here at this mill are colored—about 200 out of 700. I call 'em 'boys' whether they're white or black. I don't think of them as white and black, and *didn't* until this whole thing came up. They've got no problem registering to vote in Vicksburg. I believe 2,000-3,000 are registered in the county. Why up in Kansas City I had 250 niggers in a mill, and not 5 percent of them ever registered.

"Some of the colored boys here in the mill could be considered supervisors—they're lead men. Why, I have *fired* supervisors for abusing people. They're *people*, I say.

"Why are policemen vicious? They're underpaid. You pay low salaries, you attract a certain kind…. I know the COFO[3] office here in Vicksburg was bombed, but I don't believe any local people did it. I would guess it was done from the outside…. No, I haven't ever seen one of those COFO people.

"We had a fellow come down here from a Northern corporation to look the town over. He tells me, I like it fine down here, and I'm going to recommend we build a plant here. But he goes back North and says to his directors: we're planning to build a plant down in Mississippi, and they say: You must be crazy! Well, he tried, but he can't argue with them. That's why Vicksburg has got to change.

---

3. The Council of Federated Organizations was a civil rights umbrella group.

"Now I wouldn't tell this to everyone. But we pay for two sets of schools down here, and that's why we can't afford to pay good wages to teachers. And so we're not getting good teachers like we had when I was a kid."

* * *

At the COFO "office" in Vicksburg, an old frame house deep in the Negro part of town, cluttered with mimeographed announcements, the walls covered by posters and clippings and home-made signs, fifteen or so Negro high school youngsters were listening to some jazz records. One sat in a corner, typing. Three others, "the staff," sat at a table with me and talked.

There had been two bombings in the past week in Vicksburg. One was the Anderson Café, used by COFO workers. No one was hurt there. The other was the Vicksburg Café, owned by a white man downtown, and once boycotted because it would not admit Negroes. Three months ago it was integrated, and a week before the bombing three whites beat up a Negro there. Then came the fire bomb. A Negro waitress tried to jump behind the counter to escape the flames and broke both her arms.

The three young Negro staff fellows—all eighteen or nineteen—were from different towns in Mississippi: Vicksburg, McComb, Drew. One was a SNCC man, one was a CORE man, and one, chuckling, said he was a combination of SNCC and CORE. They agreed the NAACP had been in Vicksburg since

1919 and hadn't done much of anything. All were veterans of boycotts, of demonstrations, of jail. No, there was no Freedom School operating in Vicksburg now. They had started one in the summer, but last October it was destroyed by a bomb, and its library with it. Fifteen people were there at the time, but no one was seriously hurt. A baby was scratched, and one lady's leg was cut.

There were two rooms in back, the walls lined with books, and cases of books crisscrossing the floor. There were 7,000 books, donated by people all over the United States, and 1,000 were out on loan. (The city library had been open only to whites until a month ago.) In the spaces between the bookcases were bare mattresses. Staff people slept there, and one was stretched out on a mattress as we walked through. Since the bombing, they were maintaining a twenty-four-hour vigil.

A white girl walked in. She had spent last summer in Florida with a CORE task force on voter registration; during her winter break from the University of Rochester she had come down to Vicksburg. Had been here now seventy-three days ("Yes," she smiled. "I count them.") She'd just come from a meeting of Negro women. She was tutoring one high school senior in math. She took me to visit Mrs. Dilla Irwin, a Negro woman who was editing a newspaper born out of the Mississippi Summer Project of 1964, the *Vicksburg Citizens' Appeal*.

Mrs. Irwin turned from her typewriter: "I was born in Vicksburg, and hatred sort of grew in me as I listened to my father and mother talking. I had seven brothers, and I remember after we got up to some size they were told to call other white boys, their own age, mister, and sir.

"I recall my first fear, when I was seven or eight years old. Parents were driving one night from church on this horse-drawn buggy, a beautiful night, those big cannon from the memorial gleaming on the highway. All at once someone said halt, all these men with guns. They asked Daddy about some Negro man who was a friend of a colored woman who had killed a white man. We got out of it all right. But that fear stayed.

"My dad was a sharecropper, and I lived in the Delta as a child, went to high school here in Vicksburg, got into fights with white kids. Then I went to live with my older sister in Chicago during the Second World War, and went to Northwestern night school, school of journalism, also a teachers college at night. Worked in defense plants in the day

"I got married in Chicago, have one son who volunteered for the army when he was seventeen. Now he's twenty-one and in Vietnam. Was always proud to be in the service. But the other day I got a letter from him asking if it was true what was happening in Alabama, and if so, what am I fighting for, he said."

* * *

On March 1, 1965, the eight-page *Vicksburg Citizens' Appeal*, an attractive, photo-offset paper, tabloid size, ran its lead story on a countywide meeting of the Freedom Democratic Party, where people from different precincts discussed problems they wanted to solve: poorly surfaced county roads, overcrowded schools, unequal welfare payments, drainage ditches overflowing with sewage onto people's land because of lack of pipe sewers. People spoke of needing gas and electricity, and new fireplugs.

Another story told of a continuing boycott of schools in Issaquena and Sharkey Counties in another part of the Delta, with five Freedom Schools set up there for students staying out of class. The boycott had begun a month before when 181 students were suspended from school for wearing Freedom buttons.

There were two editorials in that issue. One was on the role of Negro ministers: "The Negroes have always respected the minister and looked to him for guidance. He has, since Reconstruction, been a symbol of leadership to his people. Where is this leadership that is so sorely needed at this time?... Preparing souls for life in heaven is very good. However, some thought should be given to life on earth."

The *Appeal* printed an essay written by a high school boy:

> Life is real, life is honest, and the grave is not its goal.... I as a Negro teen-ager am interested in people whether they be Negro, Chinese, Jew, Indian, white, Mexican, Spanish.... The color of my skin in Southern America sets me aside from the general treatment of humanity. My life is a keep quiet; my thoughts are hidden secrets.
>
> Can I forever live as a bird in a cage? When will the door be opened? As I view the situation in Mississippi I

can truly see a bird's cage with tiny little Negro birds flying around in it. I can see the feeders with their little sacks of food. I see Governor Paul Johnson as he pours a little bit of prosperity into the trough of my cage. I see Mr. Ross Barnett as he removes the waste from my cage.

But I, one little happy bird, am ready to fly out of my cage and enjoy the sweetness of freedom.

BOSTON, MASSACHUSETTS. Anthropologists say the world at any moment shows all the stages of its evolution; and so the South now reveals every trait of past and future. Diverse currents flow, mix, collide there: the Negro, the white, the national government, the Northerner, the world beyond the seas.

Negroes, a century ago, crept out cautiously over the battle ruins but, except for a few bold figures, did not move far from slavery. Northern and Southern politicians one year bid them forward, the next pushed them back.

In 1965, however, the initiative is with the Negro militant, and everyone in the nation watches nervously for the next move. The lady in the cabin outside Lynchburg waits, as did the non-rebelling slave, but she waits on a moving belt, pulled by the bodies of black youngsters in Mississippi and Alabama, by the brave ones of the Student Nonviolent Coordinating Committee, by the high school student in Vicksburg ready to fly out of his cage. In a Mississippi Freedom School in the summer of 1964, Negro youngsters read *Portrait of the Artist as a Young Man*, in which Joyce wrote:

The spell of arms and voices: the white arms of roads, their promise of close embraces and the black arms of tall ships that stand against the moon, their tale of distant nations.... And the air is thick with their company as they call to me, their kinsman, making ready to go, shaking the wings of their exultant and terrible youth.

To the dark burst of feeling, the half-uttered thoughts of the Negro, Southern white men respond in confusion. Some pick up guns, as did their ancestors in gray, but their chance died at Gettysburg, and the murders they commit only quicken the pace of change. Most mutter and complain, but inch by inch make peace with the encroaching new order. A few of the young ones give a new kind of rebel cry, one of protest against the sins of their fathers, and they join black boys and girls of their own age, mingling their accents and their dreams (Two hundred of them, white college students from Tennessee to Mississippi, gathered in Atlanta in the fall of 1964, planning their assault on the past.)

The salesman from South Carolina keeps his eye on the morning newspaper and the business ledger, preparing to roll with the tide. He has traveled, seen the North, and knows, or perhaps just senses, that once the furor is over his daughter won't really marry a nigra, will probably not even go to school with one; that a business society which makes the gestures of equality need not be overturned.

The national government behaves very much as it did in the time of Lincoln, with that priority system which all governments everywhere dutifully observe: "Union first, freedom second." As

Lincoln with the Abolitionists, it is sensitive; it trims and heels with the gusts of protest. One hundred years after the Emancipation Proclamation, ten years after the beginning of the Negro Revolt in Montgomery, thirty days after policemen began swinging their clubs against human heads in Selma, Alabama, there came the first forthright presidential plea for racial justice couched in the language of morality rather than expediency.

And the legislative machinery began cranking out still another civil rights bill, the fourth in eight years. Continued fire-bombings, beatings, jailings, in Alabama, Mississippi, Georgia, Louisiana, indicated none of this would be enough. Yet no atrocity, not even the organized murder of three young civil rights workers in Mississippi in 1964, seems able to induce the President to invoke his statutory powers to set up a permanent protective force of special agents in the South to guard citizens against both private and official violence. The federal government will use the ordinary, slow processes of litigation and legislation on behalf of Negro rights, and, on extraordinary occasions, to call out the army for short-term duty. But, perhaps knowing the American citizenry is moved only by major disaster, the President chooses not to take preventive action against the intimidation and terrorism that is recorded by the hour in matter-of-fact SNCC field reports. In the matter of racial equality, the Administration remains, as always, a liberal government, and therefore a minimum government.

The white North reacts with horror at murder in the South, with indifference at the less dramatic, daily pain of poverty and fear, with trepidation at Negroes pushing too fast into their neighborhoods and schools. People approach their government as politicians, not citizens, considering what is *practical* over what is right. Politics itself becomes the art of the probable. The limits to change in Atlanta and Birmingham can be seen in New York, Chicago and Washington, DC.

What begins to disturb the North now is that thousands of its youngsters—college students mostly—are straining to look beyond these limits. They go South to walk hand in hand with young black radicals. They come back with a deep irreverence for everything whose worth has been established over centuries. A Radcliffe girl wrote from Gulfport, Mississippi, in the summer of 1964: "For the first time in my life, I am seeing what it is like to be poor, oppressed, and hated. And what I see here does not apply only to Gulfport or to Mississippi or even to the South."

"The world is coming in on the South," said the white businessman from South Carolina, and he was understating the reality. At a meeting on the Mississippi Gulf Coast, a young Negro SNCC worker told me: "You know, I saw one of those Vietcong guerrillas on TV the other day. He was ragged, angry, dark-skinned, and poor. I swear he looked just like one of us!" The revolution of the hungry is rising on all sides, in Asia, Africa and, frighteningly close, in Latin America, and we are just beginning to understand that it is more awesome, more inexorable, than communism.

That revolution's only representatives in the United States are young Negroes offering their bodies in the Deep South. They may eventually be isolated and crushed, or simply absorbed into the mainstream of moderate American reform; these are the two traditional ways of dealing with dangerous movements in this country. Or, with some special strength, gathered from like people in other parts of the world, they may yet fan a flame of change through this nation.

In the ramshackle COFO office in Vicksburg, Mississippi, someone had copied some lines from Christopher Fry and tacked them on the wall:

> Dark and cold we may be, but this
> is no winter now. The frozen misery
> of centuries breaks, cracks, begins to move,
> the thunder is the thunder of the floes,
> the thaw, the flood, the upstart spring...
> Affairs are now soul size. ✱

VIETNAM:
SETTING THE MORAL EQUATION

JANUARY 17, 1966

When those of us who would make an end to the war speak passionately of "the moral issue" in Vietnam, only our friends seem to understand. The government continues to bomb fishing villages, shoot women, disfigure children by fire or explosion, while its policy brings no outcry of opposition from Hubert Humphrey, Oscar Handlin, Max Lerner or millions of others. And we wonder why.

The answer, I suggest, involves the corruption of means, the confusion of ends, the theory of the lesser evil, and the easy reversibility of moral indignation in a species which is aroused to violence by symbols. To explain all this, however, is to get involved in a discussion of dangerous questions, which many people in the protest movement avoid by talking earnestly and vacantly about "morality" in the abstract, or by burrowing energetically into military realities, legal repartee, negotiating positions and the tactics of "broad coalition." Yet it is only by discussing root questions of means and ends—questions such as violence, revolution and alternative social systems—that we can understand what it means to say there is "a moral issue" in Vietnam.

To start with, we ought to recognize the escalation of evil means during this century—a process in which few of us can claim innocence. What Hitler did was to extend the already approved doctrine of indiscriminate mass murder (10 million dead on the battlefields of World War I) to its logical end, and thus stretch further than ever before the limits of the tolerable. By killing one-third of the world's Jews, the Nazis diminished the horror of any atrocity that was separated by two degrees of fiendishness from theirs. (Discussing with one of my students Hochhuth's *The Deputy*, I asked if we were not all deputies today, watching the bombing of Vietnamese villages; she replied, no, because this is not as bad as what Hitler did.)

The Left still dodges the problem of violent means to achieve just ends. (This is not true of Herbert Marcuse and Barrington Moore in the book they have done with Robert Wolff: A *Critique of Pure Tolerance*. But it was so true of the Communists in the United States that the government, in the Smith Act trials, had to distort the facts in order to prove that the Communists would go as far as Thomas Jefferson in the use of revolutionary violence.) To ignore this question, both by avoiding controversy about comparative social systems as ends, and forgoing discussion of violence as a means, is to fail to create a rational basis for moral denunciation of our government's actions in Vietnam.

I would start such a discussion from the supposition that it is logically indefensible to hold to an absolutely nonviolent position, because it is at least theoretically conceivable that a small violence might be required to prevent a larger one. Those who are immediately offended by this statement should consider World War II, the assassination attempt on Hitler, the American, French, Russian, Chinese, Cuban revolutions, possible armed revolt in South Africa, the case of Rhodesia, the Deacons in Louisiana.[4] Keep in mind that many who support the war in Vietnam may do so on grounds which they believe similar to those used in the above cases.

The terrible thing is that once you stray from absolute nonviolence you open the door for the most shocking abuses. It is like distributing scalpels to an eager group, half of whom are surgeons and half butchers. But that is man's constant problem—how to release the truth without being devoured by it.

How can we tell butchers from surgeons, distinguish between a healing and a destructive act of violence? The first requirement

---

4.   The Deacons for Defense and Justice was an armed black self-defense organization that inspired later groups like the Black Panthers.

is that our starting point must always be nonviolence, and that the burden of proof, therefore, is on the advocate of violence to show, with a high degree of probability, that he is justified. In modern American civilization, we demand unanimity among twelve citizens before we will condemn a single person to death, but we will destroy thousands of people on the most flimsy of political assumptions (like the domino theory of revolutionary contagion).

What proof should be required? I suggest four tests:

(1)   Self-defense, against outside attackers or a counterrevolutionary force within, using no more violence than is needed to repel the attack, is justified. This covers that Negro housewife who several years ago in a little Georgia town, at home alone with her children, fired through the door at a gang of white men carrying guns and chains, killing one, after which the rest fled. It would sacrifice the Rhineland to Hitler in 1936, and even Austria (for the Austrians apparently preferred not to fight), but demands supporting the Loyalist government in Spain, and defending Czechoslovakia in 1938. And it applies to Vietnamese fighting against American attackers who hold the strings of a puppet government.

(2) Revolution is justified, for the purpose of overthrowing a deeply entrenched oppressive regime, unshakable by other means. Outside aid is permissible (because rebels, as in the American Revolution, are almost always at a disadvantage against the holders of power), but with the requirement that the manpower for the revolution be indigenous, for this in itself is a test of how popular the

revolution is. This could cover the French, American, Mexican, Russian, Chinese, Cuban and Algerian cases. It would also cover the Vietcong rebellion. And a South African revolt, should it break out.

(3) Even if one of the above conditions is met, there is no moral justification for visiting violence on the innocent. Therefore, violence in self-defense or in revolution must be focused on the evil-doers, and limited to that required to achieve the goal, resisting all arguments that extra violence might speed victory. This rules out the strategic bombing of German cities in World War II, the atom bombing of Hiroshima and Nagasaki; it rules out terrorism against civilians even in a just revolution. Violence even against the guilty, when undertaken for sheer revenge, is unwarranted, which rules out capital punishment for any crime. The requirement of focused violence makes nonsensical the equating of the killing of village chiefs in South Vietnam by the Vietcong and the bombing of hospitals by American fliers; yet the former is also unjustified if it is merely an act of terror or revenge and not specifically required for a change in the social conditions of the village.

(4) There is an additional factor which the conditions of modern warfare make urgent. Even if all three of the foregoing principles are met, there is a fourth which must be considered if violence is to be undertaken: the costs of self-defense or social change must not be so high, because of the intensity or the prolongation of violence, or because of the risk of proliferation, that the victory is not worth the cost. For the Soviets to defend Cuba

from attack—though self-defense was called for—would not have been worth a general war; for the United States to defend Hungary from attack—though self-defense was called for—would not have been worth a general war. For China or Soviet Russia to aid the Vietcong with troops, though the Vietcong cause is just, would be wrong if it seriously risked a general war. Under certain conditions, nations should be captive rather than be destroyed, or revolutionaries should bide their time. Indeed, because of the omnipresence of the great military powers—the United States and the USSR (perhaps this is not so true for the countries battling England, France, Holland, Belgium, Portugal)—revolutionary movements may have to devise tactics short of armed revolt to overturn an oppressive regime.

The basic principle I want to get close to is that violence is most clearly justified when those whose own lives are at stake make the decision on whether the prize is worth dying for. Self-defense and guerrilla warfare, by their nature, embody this decision. Conscript armies and unfocused warfare violate it. And no one has a right to decide that someone else is better off dead than Red, or that someone else should die to defend his way of life, or that an individual (like Norman Morrison[5]) should choose to live rather than die.

---

5.   Morrison was a 31-year-old Quaker who in November 1965 immolated himself below Secretary of Defense Robert MacNamara's Pentagon office in protest of the Vietnam War.

It would be foolish to pretend that this summary can be either precise or complete. Those involved in self-defense or in a revolution need no intellectual justification; their emotions reflect some inner rationality. It is those outside the direct struggle, deciding whether to support one side or to stay out, who need to think clearly about principles. Americans, therefore, possessing the greatest power and being furthest removed from the problems of self-defense or revolution, need thoughtful deliberation most. All we can do in social analysis is to offer rough guides to replace non-thinking, to give the beginnings of some kind of moral calculus.

However, it takes no close measurement to conclude that the American bombings in Vietnam, directed as they are to farming areas, villages, hamlets, fit none of the criteria listed, and so are deeply immoral, whatever else is true about the situation in Southeast Asia or the world. The silence of the government's supporters on this—from Hubert Humphrey to the academic signers of advertisements—is particularly shameful, because it requires no surrender of their other arguments to concede that this is unnecessary bestiality.

Bombings aside, none of the American military activity against the Vietcong could be justified unless it was helping a determined people to defend itself against an outside attacker. That is why the Administration, hoping to confirm by verbal repetition what cannot be verified in fact, continually uses the term "aggression" to describe the Vietnamese guerrilla activities. The expert evidence, however, is overwhelming on this question.

(1)   Philippe Devillers, the French historian, says "the insurrection existed before the Communists decided to take part.... And even among the Communists, the initiative did not originate in Hanoi, but from the grass roots, where the people were literally driven by Diem to take up arms in self-defense."

(2)   Bernard Fall says "anti-Diem guerrillas were active long before infiltrated North Vietnamese elements joined the fray."

(3)   The correspondent for *Le Monde* Jean Lacouture (in *Le Viet Nam entre deux paix*) confirms that local pressure, local conditions led to guerrilla activity.

(4)   Donald S. Zagoria, a specialist on Asian communism at Columbia University, wrote recently that it is reasonably clear that we are dealing with an indigenous insurrection in the South, and that this, not Northern assistance, is the main trouble."

One test of "defense against aggression" is the behavior of the official South Vietnamese Army—the "defenders" themselves. We find a high rate of desertions, a need to herd villagers into concentration-camp "strategic hamlets" in order to control them, the use of torture to get information from other South Vietnamese, whom you might expect to be enthusiastic about "defending" their country, and all of this forcing the United States to take over virtually the entire military operation in Vietnam.

The ordinary people of Vietnam show none of the signs of a nation defending itself against "aggression," except in their noncooperation with the government and the Americans. A hundred thousand Vietnamese farmers were conducting a rebellion with mostly captured weapons. Then they matched the intrusion of 150,000 American troops with 7,500 North Vietnamese soldiers (in November, 1965, American military officials estimated that five regiments of North Vietnamese, with 1,500 in each regiment, were in South Vietnam). Weapons were acquired from Communist countries, but not a single plane to match the horde of American bombers filling the skies over Vietnam. This adds up not to North Vietnamese aggression (if indeed North Vietnamese can be considered outsiders at all) but to American aggression, with a puppet government fronting for American power.

Thus, there is no valid principle on which the United States can defend either its bombing, or its military presence, in Vietnam. It is the factual emptiness of its moral claim which then leads it to seek a one-piece substitute, that comes prefabricated with its own rationale, surrounded by an emotional aura sufficient to ward off inspectors. This transplanted fossil is the Munich analogy, which, speaking with all the passion of Churchill in the Battle of Britain, declares: to surrender in Vietnam is to do what Chamberlain did at Munich; that is why the villagers must die.

The great value of the Munich analogy to the Strangeloves is that it captures so many American liberals, among many others. It backs the Vietnamese expedition with a coalition broad enough to include Barry Goldwater, Lyndon Johnson, George Meany and John Roche (thus reversing World War II's coalition, which excluded the far Right and included the radical Left). This bloc justifies the carnage in Vietnam with a huge image of invading armies, making only one small change in the subtitle replacing the word "Fascist" with the word "Communist." Then, the whole savage arsenal of World War II—the means both justified and unjustifiable—supported by that great fund of indignation built against the Nazis, can be turned to the uses of the American Century.

To leave the Munich analogy intact, to fail to discuss communism and fascism, is to leave untouched the major premise which supports the present policy of near genocide in Vietnam. I propose here at least to initiate such a discussion.

Let's refresh our memories on what happened at Munich. Chamberlain of England and Daladier of France met Hitler and Mussolini (this was September 30, 1938) and agreed to surrender the Sudeten part of Czechoslovakia, inhabited by German-speaking people, hoping thus to prevent a general war in Europe. Chamberlain returned to England, claiming he had brought "peace in our time." Six months later, Hitler had gobbled up the rest of Czechoslovakia; then he began presenting ultimatums to Poland, and by September 3, 1939, general war had broken out in Europe.

There is strong evidence that if the Sudetenland had not been surrendered at Munich—with it went Czechoslovakia's powerful fortifications, 70 percent of its iron, steel and electric power, 86 percent of its chemicals, 66 percent of its coal—and had Hitler then gone to war, he would have been defeated quickly, with the aid of Czechoslovakia's thirty-five well-trained divisions. And if he chose, at the sign of resistance, not to go to war, then at least he would have been stopped in his expansion.

And so, the analogy continues, to let the Communist-dominated National Liberation Front win in South Vietnam (for the real obstacle in the sparring over negotiations is the role of the NLF[6] in a new government) is to encourage more Communist expansion in Southeast Asia and beyond, and perhaps lead to a war more disastrous than the present one, to stop communism in South Vietnam is to discourage its expansion elsewhere.

We should note, first, some of the important differences between the Munich situation in 1938 and Vietnam today.

(1) In 1938, the main force operating against the Czech status quo was an outside force, Hitler's Germany, the supporting force was the Sudeten group inside led by Konrad Henlein. Since 1958 (and traceable back to 1942), the major force operating against the status quo in South Vietnam has been an inside force, formed in 1960 into the NTT, the chief supporter is not an outside nation but another part of the same nation, North Vietnam. The largest outside force in Vietnam consists of the American troops (who, interestingly, are referred to in West Germany as *Banden-kampfverbande*, Bandit Fighting Units, the name used in World War II by the Waffen-SS units to designate the guerrillas whom

---

6. The National Liberation Front, also known as the Viet Cong, fought for the liberation of South Vietnam.

they specialized in killing). To put it another way, in 1938, the Germans were trying to take over part of another country. Today, the Vietcong are trying to take over part of their own country. In 1938, the outsider was Germany. Today it is the United States.

(2)   The Czech government, whose interests the West surrendered to Hitler in 1938, was a strong, effective, prosperous, democratic government—the government of Benes and Masaryk. The South Vietnamese government, which we support, is a hollow shell of a government, unstable, unpopular, corrupt, a dictatorship of bullies and torturers, disdainful of free elections and representative government (recently they opposed establishing a National Assembly on the ground that it might lead to communism), headed by a long line of tyrants from Bao Dai to Diem to Ky, who no more deserve to be ranked with Benes and Masaryk than Governor Wallace of Alabama deserves to be compared with Robert E. Lee. It is a government whose perpetuation is not worth the loss of a single human life.

(3)   Standing firm in 1938 meant engaging, in order to defeat once and for all, the central threat of that time, Hitler's Germany. Fighting in Vietnam today, even if it brings total victory, does not at all engage what the United States considers the central foes— the Soviet Union and Communist China. Even if international communism *were* a single organism, to annihilate the Vietcong would be merely to remove a toenail from an elephant. To engage what we think is the source of our difficulties (Red China one day, Soviet Russia the next) would require nuclear war, and even Rob-

ert Strange McNamara doesn't seem up to that.

(4) There is an important difference between the historical context of Munich, 1938, and that of Vietnam, 1966. Munich was the culmination of a long line of surrenders and refusals to act: when Japan invaded China in 1931, when Mussolini invaded Ethiopia in 1935, when Hitler remilitarized the Rhineland in 1936, when Hitler and Mussolini supported the Franco attack on Republican Spain 1936-39, when Japan attacked China in 1937, when Hitler took Austria in the spring of 1938. The Vietnam crisis, on the other hand, is the culmination of a long series of events in which the West has on occasion held back (as in Czechoslovakia in 1948, or Hungary in 1956), but more often taken firm action, from the Truman Doctrine to the Berlin blockade, to the Korean conflict, to the Cuban blockade of 1962. So, withdrawing from Vietnam would not reinforce a pattern in the way that the Munich pact did. It would be another kind of line in that jagged graph which represents recent foreign policy.

(5) We have twenty years of Cold War history to test the proposition derived from the Munich analogy—that a firm stand in Vietnam is worth the huge loss of life, because it will persuade the Communists there must be no more uprisings elsewhere. But what effect did our refusal to allow the defeat of South Korea (1950-53), or our aid in suppressing the Huk rebellion in the Philippines (1947-55), or the suppression of guerrillas in Malaya (1948-60), have on the guerrilla warfare in South Vietnam which

started around 1958 and became consolidated under the National Liberation Front in 1960? If our use of subversion and arms to overthrow Guatemala in 1954 showed the Communists in Latin America that we meant business, then how did it happen that Castro rebelled and won in 1959? Did our invasion of Cuba in 1961, our blockade in 1962, show other revolutionaries in Latin America that they must desist? Then how explain the Dominican uprising in 1965? And did our dispatch of Marines to Santo Domingo end the fighting of guerrillas in the mountains of Peru?

One touches the Munich analogy and it falls apart. This suggests something more fundamental: that American policy makers and their supporters simply do not understand either the nature of communism or the nature of the various uprisings that have taken place in the postwar world. They are not able to believe that hunger, homelessness, oppression are sufficient spurs to revolution, without outside instigation, just as Dixie governors could not believe that Negroes marching in the streets were not led by outside agitators.

So, communism and revolution require discussion. They are sensitive questions, which some in the protest movement hesitate to broach for fear of alienating allies. But they are basic to that inversion of morality which enables the United States to surround the dirty war in Vietnam with the righteous glow of the war against Hitler.

A key assumption in this inversion is that communism and Nazism are sufficiently identical to be treated alike. However, communism as a set of ideals has attracted good people—not racists or bullies or militarists—all over the world. One may argue that in Communist countries citizens had better affirm their allegiance to it, but that doesn't account for the fact that millions in France, Italy and Indonesia are Communist Party members, that countless others all over the world have been inspired by Marxian ideals. And why should they not? These ideals include peace, brotherhood, racial equality, the classless society, the withering away of the state.

If Communists behave much better out of power than in it, that is a commentary not on their ideals but on weaknesses which they share with non-Communist wielders of power. If, presumably in pursuit of their ideals, they have resorted to brutal tactics, maintained suffocating bureaucracies and rigid dogmas, that makes them about as reprehensible as other nations, other social systems which, while boasting of the Judeo-Christian heritage, have fostered war, exploitation, colonialism and race hatred. We judge ourselves by our ideals, others by their actions. It is a great convenience.

The ultimate values of the Nazis, let us recall, included racism, elitism, militarism and war as ends in themselves. Unlike either the Communist nations or the capitalist democracies, there is here no ground for appeal to higher purposes. The ideological basis for coexistence between Communist and capitalist nations is the rough consensus of ultimate goals which they share. While war is held off, the citizens on both sides—it is to be hoped and indeed it is beginning to occur—will increasingly insist that their leaders live up to these values.

One of these professed values—which the United States is trying with difficulty to conceal by fragile arguments and feeble analogies—is the self-determination of peoples. Self-determination justifies the overthrow of entrenched oligarchies—whether foreign or domestic—in ways that will not lead to general war. China, Egypt, Indonesia, Algeria and Cuba are examples. Such revolutions tend to set up dictatorships, but they do so in the name of values which can be used to erode that same dictatorship. They therefore deserve as much general support and specific criticism as did the American revolutionaries, who set up a slave-holding government, but with a commitment to freedom which later led it, *against its wishes*, to abolitionism.

The easy use of the term "totalitarian" to cover both Nazis and Communists, or to equate the South Vietnamese regime with that of Ho Chi Minh, fails to make important distinctions, just as dogmatists of the Left sometimes fail to distinguish between Fascist states and capitalist democracies.

This view is ahistorical on two counts. First, it ignores the fact that, for the swift economic progress needed by new nations today, a Communist-led regime does an effective job (though it is not the only type of new government that can). In doing so, it raises educational and living standards and thus paves the way (as the USSR and Eastern Europe already show) for attacks from within on its own thought-control system. Second, this view forgets that the United States and Western Europe, now haughty in prosperity, with a fair degree of free expression, built their present status on the backs of either slaves or colonial people, and subjected their own laboring populations to several generations of misery before beginning to look like welfare states.

The perspective of history suggests that a united Vietnam under Ho Chi Minh is preferable to the elitist dictatorship of the South, just as Maoist China with all its faults is preferable to the rule of Chiang, and Castro's Cuba to Batista's. We do not have pure choices in the present, although we should never surrender those values which can shape the future. Right now, for Vietnam, a Communist government is probably the best avenue to that whole packet of human values which make up the common morality of mankind today: the preservation of human life, self-determination, economic security, the end of race and class oppression, that freedom of speech which an educated population begins to demand.

This is a conclusion which critics of government policy have hesitated to make. With some, it is because they simply don't believe it, but with others, it is because they don't want to rock the boat of "coalition." Yet the main obstacle to United States withdrawal is a fear that is real—that South Vietnam will then go Communist. If we fail to discuss this honestly, we leave untouched a major plank in the structure that supports US action.

When the jump is made from real fears to false ones, we get something approaching lunacy in American international behavior.

Richard Hofstadter, in *The Paranoid Style in American Politics*, writes of "the central preconception of the paranoid style—the existence of a vast, insidious, preternaturally effective international conspiratorial network designed to perpetrate acts of the most fiendish character."

Once, the center of the conspiracy was Russia. A political scientist doing strategic research for the government told me recently with complete calm that his institute decided not too long ago that they had been completely wrong about the premise which underlay much of American policy in the postwar period—the premise that Russia hoped to take over Western Europe by force. Yet now, with not a tremor of doubt, the whole kit and caboodle of the invading-hordes theory is transferred to China.

Paranoia starts from a base of facts, but then leaps wildly to an absurd conclusion. It is a fact that China is totalitarian in its limitation of free expression, is fierce in its expressions of hatred for the United States, that it crushed opposition in Tibet, and fought for a strip of territory on the Indian border. But let's consider India briefly: it crushed an uprising in Hyderabad, took over the state of Kerala, initiated attacks on the China border, took Goa by force, and is fierce in its insistence on Kashmir. Yet we do not accuse it of wanting to take over the world.

Of course, there is a difference. China is emotionally tied to and sometimes aids obstreperous rebellions all over the world. However, China is not the source of these rebellions. The problem is not that China wants to take over the world, but that various peoples want to take over their parts of the world, and without the courtesies that attend normal business transactions. What if the Negroes in Watts really rose up and tried to take over Los Angeles? Would we blame that on Castro?

Not only does paranoia lead the United States to see international conspiracy where there is a diversity of Communist nations based on indigenous Communist movements. It also confuses communism with a much broader movement of this century—the rising of hungry and harassed people in Asia, Africa, Latin America (and the American South). Hence we try to crush radicalism in one place (Greece, Iran, Guatemala, the Philippines, etc.) and apparently succeed, only to find a revolution—whether Communist or Socialist or nationalist or of indescribable character—springing up somewhere else. We surround the world with our navy, cover the sky with our planes, fling our money to the winds, and then a revolution takes place in Cuba, 90 miles from home. We see every rebellion everywhere as the result of some devilish plot concocted in Moscow or Peking, when what is really happening is that people everywhere want to eat and to be free, and will use desperate means and any one of a number of social systems to achieve their ends.

The other side makes the same mistake. The Russians face a revolt in Hungary or Poznan, and attribute it to bourgeois influence, or to American scheming. Stalin's paranoia led him to send scores of old Bolsheviks before the firing squad. The Chinese seem to be developing obsessions about the United States, but in their case we are doing our best to match their wildest accusations with reality. It would be paranoid for Peking to claim that the United States is surrounding China with military bases, occupying countries on its border, keeping hundreds of thousands of troops within striking distance, contemplating the bombing of its population—if it were not largely true.

A worldwide revolution is taking place, aiming to achieve the very values that all major countries, East and West, claim to uphold: self-determination, economic security, racial equality, freedom. It takes many forms—Castro's, Mao's, Nasser's, Sukarno's, Senghor's, Kenyatta's. That it does not realize all its aims from the start makes it hardly more imperfect than we were in 1776. The road to freedom is stony, but people are going to march along it. What we need to do is improve the road, not blow it up.

The United States government has tried hard to cover its moral nakedness in Vietnam. But the signs of its failure grow by the day. Facts have a way of coming to light. Also, we have recently had certain experiences which make us less naïve about governments while we become more hopeful about people: the civil rights movement, the student revolt, the rise of dissent inside the Communist countries, the emergence of fresh, brave spirits in Africa, Asia, Latin America, and in our own country.

It is not our job, as citizens, to point out the difficulties of our military position (this, when true, is quite evident), or to work out clever bases for negotiating (the negotiators, when they must, will find a way), or to dissemble what we know is true in order to build a coalition (coalitions grow naturally from what is common to a heterogeneous group, and require each element to represent its colors as honestly as possible to make the mosaic accurate and strong). As a sign of the strange "progress" the world has made, from now on all moral transgressions take the form of irony, because they are committed against officially proclaimed values. The job of citizens, in any society, any time, is simply to point this out. ✳

EMANCIPATION FROM DOGMA: THE OLD LEFT AND THE NEW

APRIL 4, 1966

There was an American Left in the thirties. Then the country went through a World War and a Cold War, reconversion, McCarthyism and prosperity, and for a time there was not in this country much that could reasonably be called leftist. Now in the sixties the New Left has emerged. It bears some resemblance to the radicalism of the thirties, but what follows here will be primarily an exercise in contrasts.

It is all too easy to be witty in describing of the militant Left of the 1930s—the stage whispering, the posturing, the dogma, the in-fighting, the Talmudic debates among Trotskyists, Communists, Lovestonites, old Wobblies; the hypocrisy, the self-righteousness. But measure these defects against the evils which the Left saw in the thirties, the hungry children, the evicted families shivering in the streets, the men standing in long lines for a day's work, the Negroes lynched in the South and jammed into filthy ghettos in the North. All this happening in the richest nation, the most liberal nation, in the world. And overseas, the Japanese butchering China, Mussolini's tanks rumbling toward Ethiopian farmers carrying spears, German warplanes bombing Barcelona, Hitler beginning the deadly roundup of the Jews and raving in the Berlin *Sportspalast*. And all this happening while Western Christian countries hemmed and hawed and murmured about communism. The old Left may have been a movement of Don Quixotes, but it pointed out the crimes, here and abroad, before anyone else.

In the Roosevelt circle itself there was no one we could call a militant leftist, despite the cries of the Chamber of Commerce, Father Coughlin and the Liberty League; despite Al Smith's assertion that behind the New Dealers were really Norman Thomas, Karl Marx and Lenin. Rexford Guy Tugwell, of all in the inner Roosevelt group, was the boldest in his economic analysis. As early as 1932, in a paper to the American Economic Association, he called for national economic planning and the control of prices and profits—which meant, he said, that "business will logically be required to disappear."

We would need to move outside the Roosevelt official family to find leftist intellectuals in any number. There was John Dewey, whose pragmatism went beyond that of FDR to embrace an attack on the profit system. There was Upton Sinclair, with his mild, homey, American brand of socialism, who said that "in a cooperative society every man, woman and child would have the equivalent of $5,000 a year income from the labor of the able-bodied young men for three or four hours per day." Reinhold Niebuhr urged that "private ownership of the productive processes" be abandoned. Harvard philosopher William Ernest Hocking, asking for "collectivism of a sort," rejected the collectivism both of a "headless liberalism" and of a "heady" communism or fascism. Paul Douglas, then an economist at the University of Chicago, called for organization of the weak and poor to force FDR's hand and move him toward a bolder program.

When we speak of the *militant* Left, however, we must move from the professors to the students, from the intellectuals to the labor organizers, from the lecture platform to the picket line. We must see the demonstrations of the unemployed, the farmers violently preventing foreclosures, the workers boarding streetcars and refusing to pay fare, the neighbors who moved the furniture of evicted families back into the tenements in New York City; and those who sailed off to fight in the Spanish Civil War. And then there were those fifty-five people in Chicago who were charged with dismantling an entire four-story building and carrying it away, brick by brick!

In that crazy, billowing, tangled web of the Left, I want to single out for comparison with today's radicals one key strand—the Communist-influenced Left. The Left of the thirties was much more than that, but I have two reasons for concentrating on that segment. First, it was undoubtedly stronger, more influential than the rest. Second, the comparison with today's radicals is a more than academic exercise; it may throw light on the accusations sometimes made that the New Left is either secretly Communist, or infiltrated by Communists or sympathetic to Maoism.

The Communist Party reported 12,000 members in 1932, and about 80,000 at the end of the decade. The turnover was lively, and in the thirties perhaps 100,000 or even 200,000 Americans moved in and out of the party, so that one might say several hundred thousand were directly influenced by Communist ideas. These people worked in the more militant unions of the CIO, in the American Student Union and the American Youth Congress, in fraternal societies like the International Workers Order, in civil rights groups like the National Negro Congress, in foreign policy groups like the American League Against War and Fascism.

To represent the New Left of today, while recognizing that there are other groups which might be considered part of it, I would discuss those elements I know best: the Student Nonviolent Coordinating Committee [SNCC], which is the most aggressive of the civil rights groups working in the South; Students for a

Democratic Society [SDS], which carries on a variety of activities on campuses, in depressed urban areas, on civil rights and foreign policy; and that assorted group of intellectuals, civil rights workers and just ordinary draft-card burners who have become active in opposition to the war in Vietnam.

Before noting the differences between the old Left and the New Left, we should recognize their common ground. Both have been sharply, angrily critical of American society, at home and abroad. Both have pointed to poverty in the midst of wealth, to sins committed against the Negro, to limitations on free expression by congressional committees and public prosecutors, to shameful behavior in foreign policy. And in this, both movements—despite characteristics which I find distasteful in the old Left and mostly missing in the New Left—have made contributions to the values in American society which almost all of us claim to cherish.

I see, first, in the new militants, a lack of ideology unthinkable in the old Left. Alfred Kazin (in *Starting Out in The Thirties*) referred to many leftists of his time as "ideologues." They were always attending classes on Marxist theory, buying or selling or arguing about works by the Big Four (Marx, Engels, Lenin, Stalin), engaging in endless discussions on surplus value, dialectical materialism, the absolute impoverishment of the working class, Plekhanov's theory of the role of the individual, Stalin's views on the national question, Engels on the origin of the family, Lenin on economism, or imperialism, or social democracy or "the woman question."

The people in SNCC, by and large, know little about Marx. They have no manifesto or any other infallible guide to the truth. Their discussions are rarely theoretical, and deal mostly with day-to-day practical problems: the tent city in Lowndes County, hunger in Greenville, the Freedom Democratic Party, how to meet the next payroll for 130 field secretaries. SDS people I have met are more white than SNCC, more middle class, more intellectual, and thus have read more of Marx—but they don't seem to take it as gospel. I recently read a book of essays by SDS people, and found in it very little that was abstract, above the level of immediate issues. The old Left would have had a quotation from Lenin on the headquarters wall. In the dilapidated SNCC offices in Atlanta recently I saw:

> Ever danced out on a limb?
> It doesn't always break.
> And sometimes when it does you fall
> into a grassy meadow.

All this indicates an open-mindedness and a flexibility in the New Left that was rare in the thirties. There is a refreshing lack of pompous intellectuality, of quotations from the great, of a "line." There is an unfortunate side to this. The New Left lacks analysis of alternative tactics, systems, institutions: for instance, in the argument between Leon Keyserling and Robert Theobald on the question of working the American economic system to full capacity; or in whether public corporations or private cooperatives or nationalized enterprises would serve society best, and in what situations; or in how to work inside and outside the present two-party system; or in the problem of what institutions can substitute for the repressive state in a new society. The good side is a lack of commitment to a particular nation or system.

The old Left was rigidly committed: the nation was the Soviet Union and the system was socialism. Some adherents were disillusioned by Stalin's purges of old Bolsheviks in the thirties; others dropped away after the nonaggression pact with Germany. But many stood fast, held by the power of an earlier vow.

The new generation of radicals starts with no such oaths of loyalty. They have no illusions about the purity of any nation, any system. They have seen Stalinism unmasked—by Khrushchev himself. They have seen aggression, subversion and double-dealing on all sides, West as well as East, "free world" as well as "Communist world." They are very much aware of Russian aggression in Hungary, Chinese repression in Tibet, and the problem of power in the best of revolutions.

But they also know that the American CIA overthrew a democratically elected government in Guatemala, that the United States secretly conspired in the invasion of Cuba, that our Marines invaded the Dominican Republic in violation of the Rio Pact. They have grown up in a world where force and deception are ubiquitous, and they have developed what I believe is a healthy disposition to call the shots as they see them, no matter whose image is damaged.

The old Left was sectarian, suspicious and exclusive. The Socialists would expel Communists, the Trotskyists would expel Socialists, and the Communists would expel almost everyone. While SNCC indulges in some silly sniping at other civil rights groups, both SNCC and SDS are open organizations; they welcome anyone who will work, regardless of affiliation or ideology. One result is a succession of head-shakings and warnings from various people about Communist infiltrators (this is the liberal counterpart of Communist suspiciousness), but SNCC and SDS have remained cool to the criticism. Bob Moses of SNCC, in the fall of 1963, responded to a *Life* article in which Theodore White referred accusingly to a "penetration" of SNCC by "unidentified elements." (White seemed bashful about saying that he meant Communists.) Moses replied: "It seems to me that...we have to throw what little weight we have on the side of free association."

There is an Existential quality to current radicalism that distinguishes it sharply from the style of the thirties. Marxists are rather unhappy with Existentialism, though Jean-Paul Sartre has made an attempt to reconcile his Existentialism with his Marxism. They find the Existentialist insufficiently aware of the binding force of history, incredulous of the idea of progress, excessively emotional, stubbornly individualist. The charge of emotionalism is true, but what of it? Blaise Pascal said in his *Pensées*, in the middle of the seventeen century: "The heart has its reasons, which reason does not know...." This may seem like sentimental spirituality, so ineffective (and we demand *effectiveness* today) in a cold world of *Realpolitik*, so subversive of the ironclad reason that marks modern man and particularly the modern atheistic radical. But we must now recognize that the point of ignition of the new radicalism was the civil rights movement, and this has been an emotional movement, as anyone who ever attended a mass meeting in a Negro church of the Deep South knows. One of the contributions of the new radicalism is to show that such emotionalism is not destructive of rationality, that passion in itself is morally neutral, capable of supporting any value, and that when it is attached to a humane cause, it *contributes* to rational action. It does this because verbal discourse alone is a pale reflection of life, inadequate to convey the anguish that human beings feel; words need to be intensified by emotion if they are to describe accurately the reality of both suffering and joy.

Emotion plays not only this kind of supporting role for rational decision making; it also has an initiating role in moral decisions. The logical positivists, from Hume to Hans Reichenbach, have told us that we cannot rationally deduce first statements about what *should* be. But we may very well *feel* them; and there is a shared feeling among people about certain basic values, which should not be discarded because it cannot, in the academic sense, be "proved." We *know*, we *feel*, that peace is preferable to war, nourishment to starvation, brotherhood to enmity; that it is better to be free than in jail, better to love than to hate, better to live than to die. And yet—this is the devilish power of human communication, the curse of language—we can be taught, *rationally*, that war is preferable to peace (all we ask is a few words of explanation from those on high who know and can soothe our troubled minds); that jail is preferable to freedom (due process and judicial respectability calm our indignation); that starvation is better than nourishment (for others, of course; thus we accept the destruction of crops if they are to feed "the enemy"). There are Soviet citizens, I am sure, who *feel* that it is wrong to send two writers to jail for what they have written, but the calm, reasonable explanations go forth and the feeling is smothered. Is it any wonder that this new generation of radicals so distrusts this perversion of "reason" that they are willing to trust their emotions in deciding what is right and what is wrong"? I have quoted elsewhere one of the original SNCC organizers, a young white girl from Virginia named Jane Stembridge:

> Finally it all boils down to human relationships. It has nothing to do finally with governments. It is the question of...whether I shall go on living in isolation or whether there shall be a *we*. The student movement is not a cause...it is a collision between this one person and that one person. It is *I am going to sit beside you....* Love alone is radical. Political statements are not; programs are not; even going to jail is not.

The radicals of the thirties believed fervently in the power of historical forces, churning away, moving the world inexorably toward a glorious future. This faith came from the historical materialism of

Marxism, with its confident laying out of the stages of history. The radicals I know today do not feel thus bound by history. They accept neither the Marxist nor the biblical nor any other organizing interpretation. What they know best is the present, and they consider it malleable by the power of their own hands. When you have *made* history, when you have *forced* social change, the magic of a philosophy of history fades. In eleven years, if we date the movement from the Montgomery bus boycott of 1955, the militant youngsters of the Southern movement have moved mountains. To be sure, they have not moved them very far, but to move a mountain even a few inches gives a sense of power. "The Deep South Says Never," a journalist wrote after the Supreme Court decision. But Negroes are defying guns and subterfuge in Alabama and Mississippi, organizing their own parties, preparing to elect their own sheriffs, mayors, Congressmen. In Georgia, Negroes are sitting in the state legislature, and the expulsion of Julian Bond can be seen not only as a patriotic move to support the Vietnamese war by the freedom-loving members of the Georgia General Assembly but also as a belated outburst of anger at the sight of so many Negroes sitting in their formerly sacrosanct, all-white chamber. Southern Negroes are still poor, but they dare to strike in the Mississippi Delta against the plantation owner. They are still afraid, but not as afraid as they used to be. The active ones know that the changed atmosphere is not the result of beneficence from the succession of Great White Fathers in Washington, but of their own willingness to risk their lives, to march, to demonstrate, to go to jail—that Kennedy and Johnson did not act for them, but reacted to them. These Southern militants are off their knees, they have stretched their limbs, and are ready to do more, undeterred by notions of what history does or does not permit.

Yet when the hold of history is weakened, there ensues not only awareness of freedom but a sense of despair. This is very much in the Existentialist mood, and quite different from the radicalism of the thirties. To the old radicals, revolution was always around the corner; the proletariat was always about to rise and smite the foe, capitalism was always about to collapse in one of its periodic economic crises; every bloody nose suffered by the Left was received as another sign of reactionary desperation. The great day of socialism was never far off—though it never dawned.

The New Left is not afraid to say that it is unsure of victory. Tom Hayden, writing in *The New Republic* some weeks ago, makes no cheery predictions about how SDS will transform America; he says, "Radicalism then would go beyond the concepts of optimism and pessimism as guides to work, finding itself in working despite odds. Its realism and sanity would be grounded in nothing more than the ability to face whatever comes." Michael Harrington commented on this in a subsequent issue, and was clearly unhappy. He needs to know he will win, and right away, and so seeks desperately to create a coalition which will have in it a majority of Americans. The new radical is more in tune with Wendell Phillips, the abolitionist orator, who wrote: "The reformer is careless of numbers, disregards popularity, and deals only with ideas, conscience, and common sense.... He neither expects nor is over-anxious for immediate success." Phillips contrasted the reformer with the politician, who "dwells in an everlasting now." Similarly, James Russell Lowell wrote: "The Reformer must expect compar-ative isolation, and he must be strong enough to bear it." The new radicals derive their strength from the other side of Existentialist despair: a supreme sense of responsibility, an unrelenting activism.

The radicals of the thirties were immersed in traditional pol-itics. They ran their candidates and sought entry into legislative bodies. William Z. Foster and Earl Browder were Communist candidates for President at various times; Norman Thomas was the perennial Socialist candidate. Their suspicion of parliamenta-ry democracy did not seem very penetrating. It is a fact of Ameri-can political life that the cards are stacked against minority candi-dates in our electoral college device, and in the single-district sys-tem by which we elect Congressmen. And even if a radical should break through, mysterious things begin to happen. Socialist Victor Berger, twice elected, was excluded from Congress in 1918 and 1919. Five Socialists elected to the New York State legislature were expelled just after World War I. And when Communists began electing members to the City Council in New York under the system of proportional representation, the system was abol-ished. With all this, the Communist and Socialist Parties retained a touching faith in the ballot box.

Militants of today have worked hard in the South to register Negroes to vote, they formed the Freedom Democratic Party in Mississippi, the Black Panther Party in Alabama, and tried to oust the Mississippi Congressmen from their seats and replace them with black Mississippians. However, this vigor is accompanied by a basic mistrust of politics, and what seems to me, anyway, a sharper awareness than was shown in the thirties of the limitations of parliamentary democracy. The vote, today's radicals know, is only an occasional flicker of democracy in an otherwise elitist system, the voice of the people must therefore be manifested in other ways—by day-to-day activity, by demonstrations, by a politics of constant protest rather than by the traditional politics of the ballot.

The Left of the thirties had its organized gods: the Soviet Union, the party, the body of Marxist theory. The Left of today distrusts the crystallization of power in any form that becomes rigid and commanding. Only a few have read Robert Michels, but they seem to sense instinctively his thesis that there is an "iron law of oligarchy" in any organization, with power flowing toward the top. And so, in both SDS and SNCC, there is disparagement of leadership, a preoccupation with what is called "participatory democracy," an almost romantic notion that "the people" must decide things for themselves.

Perhaps memory and the historical records squeeze the juices out of the past, but the old Left was square. The new radicals are more cool, have more fun, are less puritanical, more irreverent. I remember, in the early days of the Atlanta student movement, Julian Bond's tiny couplet:

> Look at that gal shake that thing;
> We can't all be Martin Luther King.

In the thirties, Communists and their friends juggled deftly the categories of "just wars" and "unjust wars," using Marxist scripture and analyses from on high to help decide which was which. The Germans, Italians and Japanese were denounced for their acts of war against helpless peoples: the Russian attack on Finland was justified as a case of self-defense. World War II was unjust and imperialistic until the invasion on June 22, 1941, of the Soviet Union by Hitler; it then became a people's war. It must be said that here the Communists were very much in the modern liberal tradition: both Communists and liberals see war as an extension of the internal benevolence of the system they favor.

The New Left, on the other hand, is very much influenced by the nonviolent approach of the civil rights movement, joined to an ancient American streak of pacifism which goes back to Thoreau and the abolitionist movement. That it is not a pure nonviolence is attested by the movement's general approval of the Deacons in the Deep South, and if a revolution broke out in South Africa there would be support among the New Left for it, as there has been a good deal of sympathy for the Castro revolution in Cuba. Neither were the abolitionists pure in their pacifism; when the war came they decided to support it. I would guess that the distinctions which the New Left makes are in the first instance (that of the Deacons) between aggressive violence and self-defense; and in the second instance (South Africa, Cuba, Algeria) between traditional wars for national power and revolutionary uprisings for social goals.

While most old categories of radical thought do not neatly fit the New Left, I find a cluster of anarchist ideas at its core. There is the suspicion of organized power in any form, even the power of radical groups themselves. There is the fear of centralization, and thus a tendency for decisions to be made in the field rather than by executive committees. And there is the creation of parallel organizations inside the old structure, as a tiny fire around which people gather to keep warm, as a way of showing, rather than just talking about, what the future might be like. Hence the Freedom Parties, the Freedom Schools, the Freedom Houses, the Freedom Labor Union, the Free University, the Congress of Unrepresented People, and who knows what next. This is not the free enterpriser's rejection of national power, as was suggested recently by a writer in *The New Republic* who saw a curious similarity between the New Left and the old Right. The New Left recognizes that national power is essential for certain activities (economic planning, for instance, or protection of civil rights workers in the South). But it would maintain the organized power of citizens *outside* the government to prevent tyranny.

The militants of the thirties and those of today share a common ground of concern: the abolition of war, of poverty, of racial discrimination, of political imprisonment. Both groups look ultimately to a society where cooperation and affection would replace the scramble for money and power, while leaving the individual free to determine his own way of enjoying life and love. These are marvelously desirable ends. But the leftists of the thirties committed a deadly ethical error: they made absolutes of the means which they would use to achieve these ends—the absolutes of Marxism, the party, the Soviet Union, socialism. When the means become absolutes, then it is immediately possible, even probable, that the original ends will be forgotten or distorted. By allowing that to happen, the radicals of that day lost the chance to break new ethical ground, and . followed the example of other social currents in modern times: a loving Christ-centered religion crystallized in the church, in ritual, in dogma; liberalism crystallized in the modern parliamentary, capitalist, jingoistic state; education and intellect crystallized in the PhD, the university, the scholarly monograph and the mass media.

The militant Left of the sixties has so far been fluid and freewheeling, refusing to deify any nation, any person, any ideological system; and yet holding fast—to the point of prison, of assault, even death—to a core of beliefs about the value of the individual human being. This is not to deny that there are lapses, faults, aberrations, irrationalities, pettinesses, absurdities, or that the danger of creating absolutes is not there every moment. No one can predict what will happen tomorrow. But right now the New Left looks not only concerned but honest, open, free of icons, full of courage and, above all, *alive*. ✳

THREE PRISONERS: THE PETTY ROUTE HOME

APRIL 1, 1968

omewhere between Bangkok and Paris on the flight home, our tensions beginning to ebb, I confessed to Dan Berrigan (after all, he is a Jesuit priest) that, despite heroic efforts to match my political science colleagues on the Cynicism Scale, I had somehow retained in my bones a granule of naïveté about governments, especially my own. And this despite my recent talks to students about Machiavellianism in the contemporary world, and my entranced reading of *The Spy Who Came in From the Cold* (which can be seen as a modern-day version of William Godwin's early anarchist novel, *Caleb Williams*, where a man is viciously hunted by *all* governments). But let me explain.

The State Department had learned from Radio Hanoi that North Vietnam was about to release three captured American fliers, and had read in *The New York Times* (all this is known as Intelligence) that Hanoi had wired David Dellinger, inviting a "responsible representative" to come to Hanoi to receive the fliers. After Dellinger had phoned Father Berrigan at Cornell and me in Boston (What was his thinking? That the two of us might, with strain, make one "responsible representative"?), Ambassador-at-large Harriman's office asked for a meeting with the two emissaries before their departure. The next day, a State Department man arrived in New York, while Berrigan and I were talking with Dellinger and Tom Hayden, two veterans of the New York-to-Hanoi peace run. Hayden was also a recent escort of three prisoners of the NLF from Cambodia to the United States.

The man from State had several things on his mind. First: the government would be happy to validate our passports for travel to North Vietnam. (No thanks, we said; we don't recognize the government's right to validate or invalidate anyone's right to travel anywhere.) Second: if the Vietnamese would like some reciprocal act, perhaps the United States could release a few captured North Vietnamese sailors. (If the circumstances of the capture were similar, these men would have been picked up at Coney Island; otherwise it was *not* a parallel offer; nevertheless, we absorbed the suggestion.)

Third (this came near the end, almost as an afterthought): we might make clear to the Vietnamese that the United States would negotiate on the basis of the San Antonio formula[7], and would not require, for a cessation of bombing, that the North stop all supplies to the South—only that it not increase the present flow. (I wondered if henceforth all major international crises were to be settled by formulas made in Texas towns; it seemed to me Geneva, for all its difficulties, was more neutral than San Antonio.)

However, what was most important to the man from State—quite clearly it was his main reason for approaching us—was the question. How would we return home with the fliers? By what route? By which aircraft? We didn't really know; all we had to go by was one cablegram from Hanoi. We suggested that we would wait and see what developed when we got there. To the proposal that we and the fliers all return to the States from Vientiane, Laos, by military aircraft, Father Berrigan and I said this would not please us. The man from State then said they could provide a plane which was "as far from the military as you can get"—but he did not mean Mohawk Airlines, only another kind of government plane. Nevertheless, we tentatively agreed that the decision as to how we should go would, as far as possible, be left up to the released fliers themselves.

That Wednesday evening, January 31, we departed Kennedy Airport. The next twenty-eight hours were spent almost continuous-

7. The San Antonio formula was presented by Johnson in the fall of 1967 and reiterated at the end of March 1968, after the Tet Offensive and his withdrawal from the presidential race. The Vietnamese never rejected Johnson's terms.

ly on airplanes as we dashed halfway around the globe (Copenhagen, Frankfurt, Rome, Teheran, Karachi, Calcutta, Bangkok, Vientiane) in order to intercept the Friday flight to Hanoi via Vientiane. This was a special plane run by the International Control Commission six times a month (every Friday, every other Tuesday), departing Saigon in the morning, to Phnompenh to Vientiane to Hanoi (arriving at night), and back. We made it to Vientiane on schedule, only to be informed that the NLF offensive in Saigon had closed Tan Son Nhut airport, and kept the ICC plane from taking off.

So we spent a week in Vientiane (the next scheduled flight, Tuesday, was also canceled), waiting until the plane could manage to leave Saigon. In the meantime, we visited the North Vietnamese embassy, which offered tea, sympathy and visas to Hanoi. We visited the Cambodian embassy (beginning to think the ICC plane would never make it) to obtain transit visas for Phnompenh, because the only other way to get to Hanoi is via China, and there is a flight from Phnompenh to Canton. We also approached the Chinese embassy, for transit visas, but were tersely discouraged at the embassy gate, and turned our hopes to the more substantial Chinese mission in Phnompenh.

We talked with journalists (NBC and CBS crews had flown in from Tokyo and Seoul to record our mission). We talked with young Americans in the International Volunteer Service (these IVS people were the best informed of all; they spoke Lao or Vietnamese, lived with the villagers rather than in the sprawling American Levittown outside Vientiane, and harshly criticized United States policy in both Vietnam and Laos). We spent a day with Lao villagers, and also interviewed a Pathet Lao spokesman in Vientiane.

From time to time we met with the folk at the US embassy. (An embassy man had met us on arrival at the airport, said the ambassador would be happy to see us, but considering the "delicacy" of our position, would understand if we did not visit him.) They asked us once again if we wanted our passports validated (the last approach was: "Not even *verbally*?"), discussed the problem of the canceled ICC flights, and once more showed great concern over how the pilots would come home. Again we agreed: we would leave it to the men themselves to decide.

My first reaction to the question of the route home was to consider it rather unimportant. Yet it became evident that the United States government was much concerned, indeed (and this took me by surprise) apprehensive. Why? Did they want to get the pilots out of the deadly hands of the peace movement (Berrigan and Zinn)? That didn't seem to be the point; they offered to take us back on the same plane. Apparently, they did not want the pilots to meet the world press in an unfettered series of interviews—in Bangkok, Paris, New York, and wherever else the commercial airline would stop. Why? Did they think Radio Hanoi was accurate in describing the pilots as "repentant"? This did not seem likely. These were not reluctant conscripts but career military men who had gone through intensive training: an Air Force major, an Air Force captain, a navy lieutenant. They had been prisoners a short time (all were shot down in October, 1967). And judging from the three NLF prisoners released to Tom Hayden, the other side was either not using "repentance" as a condition for release, or had very loose criteria.

What it seemed to come down to (and all this is inference, because the embassy people never discussed their anxiety explicitly; Father Berrigan and I were scarcely viewed by them as psychiatric counselors) was worry, not about desertion or denunciation (although this was always an outside chance) but merely the possibility of embarrassment, perhaps by the men showing a bit of warmth toward the Vietnamese, or (at the worst) offering implied criticism of the bombing of the North. We who spend much of our time denouncing governments for their insensitivity to human need cannot really comprehend how delicate are the antennae of governments to any criticism, to any disturbance of the carefully constructed but frail image they hold up to the world. Thus, Dan Berrigan and I, assuming cool rationality on the part of the Leviathan, could not predict that it would remain so fiercely determined to have its way on something as minor as the route home—and even at the risk of hurting (as it turned out) its "own."

On Friday, February 9th, the ICC plane got special dispensation to take off from harassed Saigon, and arrived at Vientiane, ready to take us and a handful of others (mostly ICC personnel and their families; also an elegantly dressed young British Foreign Service officer) to Hanoi. It was a very old four-engine Boeing craft; we were told that only six of them were left in the world as of two years ago. Since then, three had crashed, including one lost with all aboard on the run from Vientiane to Hanoi (apparently shot down, but it was still a mystery).

The plane flew along a narrow, pre-arranged corridor, at prescribed altitude, at agreed-upon time and air speed (so that all those anti-aircraft batteries below would hold fire), and had a last-minute check by radio with Hanoi before take-off to make sure Hanoi was not being bombed. As we crossed the Laos-Vietnam border, the French stewardess handed out flak helmets, but it was an easy flight. Over the Hanoi airfield, a searchlight picked us out, and we were soon on the ground, received warmly by members of the Peace Committee of the Democratic Republic of Vietnam, holding out two bouquets of flowers (it is hard to be unmoved when the people who have been bombed for three years by your countrymen extend their hands). Then followed an eerie auto trip through the night into Hanoi, past bombed-out buildings, anti-aircraft crews bunched in the darkness, people on foot and on bicycles moving along the road in an endless, thick stream.

In that first get-together with the Peaceniks of Hanoi (it was like visiting friends in San Francisco: "What would you like to see while you're in town, fellows?") we hit it off right away. They were a far cry from the *apparatchiks* of East or West—a relaxed bunch, young, dressed in rough jackets, hands in pocket, great guys: Oanh, Hieu, Vann, Phan. Three spoke English; one spoke French. That first night, the airmen were mentioned briefly and then that subject disappeared from the agenda while we explored people and places in Hanoi—a fascinating, intense learning of history, politics, day-to-day living. This went on for five days, and Berrigan and I were beginning to wonder about the prisoners. On Wednesday evening, returning from one of our discussions over tea, we found our friend Oanh waiting for us at the hotel. (A composer, his casual slouch deceptive; he was unerringly efficient.) He said: "Please eat supper quickly. In one hour we will meet the three prisoners."

We drove through dark streets to the prison; it seemed, like so many other government buildings, an old French villa adapted to the new exigencies. Inside, there was the usual introductory tea session. The prison commandant read us his data on the three fliers: Maj. Norris Overly, 39, flying out of a base in South Vietnam, wife and two children in Detroit; Capt. John Black, 30, flying out of Udorn airfield in Thailand, wife and three kids in Tennessee; Lt. (jg) David Methany, flying off an aircraft carrier, 24, single.

Then we moved into another room, where Berrigan and I were seated at a small table with two of our Peace Committee buddies. Along the wall to our right was a table for the prison commandant and his interpreter. Along the wall to our left, below a photo of Ho Chi Minh, another table with three empty places. On all the tables were tea, cookies, cigarettes. Hieu whispered to us: when they come in, we will introduce you briefly. He hesitated: "Whether or not you shake hands is up to you."

There was a curtained door to our left, and a very short, very tough-looking soldier came quickly through it, followed by the three fliers, who stood behind their seats, bowed to the commandant, and sat down. Dan and I were introduced. We walked over and shook hands. Then followed an hour of what can be described only as small talk: "You fellows are looking good." (They did; they looked well fed, indeed more rounded than Dan Berrigan and me, though that is not saying much.) "Where are you from?" "Oh yes, I know that town." "Do you know so-and-so in Des Moines?" And so on. An absurd conversation under the circumstances? Perhaps.

About half an hour through our chat, Major Overly became aware that we had left the Vietnamese out of the conversation, and turned to the prison commandant with a mild apology for our immersion in American-type subjects. The commandant was gracious. He wore spectacles, and his manner was mild. But he dropped one disturbing statement into the room: "You realize that if Hanoi is bombed before you leave, we may reconsider our decision to release you." Back in the hotel later, Dan and I mused and pondered over the encounter.

Hanoi had not been bombed in our first five days there, although, from the first morning, there were alerts which sent everyone into shelters. After our return to the States, newspaper men kept referring to the "bombing pause" over Hanoi—but on those five days of "the pause" the skies were completely overcast. The day after our first meeting with the fliers, Thursday, the sun shone for the first time. And on that day, the bombers came. We crowded into a shelter with several Catholic lay leaders whom we had been visiting, and heard the bombs exploding in the outer districts of Hanoi, planes droning overhead.

We wondered later about the priorities of the American government. They knew we were in Hanoi to pick up three fliers; did it not occur to them as at least a slim possibility that to bomb Hanoi at exactly that time might endanger the release? Granted that the military objectives of the bombing were more important to the United States than any consideration for the lives of Vietnamese (with hundreds of schools, hospitals, churches destroyed; with whole villages razed, with anti-personnel bombs dropped in huge quantities, that much was clear); but were these military objectives also more important to our government than the freedom of three American fliers, who themselves had been engaged in that same military action? The insistence that the bombing should go on anyway could be seen as an admirable lack of chauvinism on the part of the US government: to it, all people, even Americans, were created equally expendable. Exactly this equalitarian ruthlessness would be revealed again (yes, *The Spy Who Came in From the Cold*) when we brought the three airmen back from Hanoi.

We prepared to leave Hanoi on Friday, the next scheduled departure of the ICC plane. This was two days after our first formal meeting with the airmen, one day after the bombing. As if to provide what scientists call a "control" on the thesis that a bombing "pause" meant bad weather, that Friday the skies were murky, and there was a "pause" over Hanoi.

In the afternoon, we met with Pham Van Dong, the Premier of North Vietnam, a man of high intelligence, oceanic calm, exuberant personal warmth (altogether a man of such stature as to make us cringe thinking of the Kys, Chiangs, Parks, Duvaliers, Humphreys and other leaders of the free world). His grasp of political realities was both firm and subtle: "Your leaders make a mistake when they think we are depending on the American peace movement. It is our own efforts, our own determination that we count on. We have no illusions about the power of the peace movement. However, it is a fact that as the war goes on, your own problems at home will intensify, and as the social issues in the United States become more difficult to solve, the war will become an intolerable burden on your society, and your people will demand that the war end, for their own sake."

Several hours before take-off from Hanoi, we "received" the three airmen from the North Vietnam Peace Committee in a little formal ceremony: Oanh made a brief statement for the committee; Dan Berrigan made one for us; Lieutenant Methany for the fliers. ("We thank the North Vietnamese government for its treatment of us.") Then we went back to the hotel, where the committee had arranged for Father Berrigan and me to have supper alone with the fliers. (Throughout, the handshake incident being only one example, they treated with sensitivity our relationship with the fliers.) The supper was splendid, served by a battery of waiters (endless bowls of hot *potage*, cold cuts, chicken, bread, beer). Methany (the youngest, blond, only a few years as a navy flier, not as sure as the other two about a military career) said, in the nearest we got to any discussion about the war: "I hope we get a chance to talk about the war with you fellows. You know, I'm a flag waver from way back; I believe in fighting to defend my country. But I hope we get to talk."

Over supper, we discussed the route home from Vientiane. We laid out the alternatives carefully: the government would probably have an army plane waiting at Vientiane; it would get the men home faster (perhaps twelve to twenty-four hours faster) than a commercial flight. (Air France could take us from Bangkok to Paris to New York, arriving Sunday noon.) It would also mean less press harassment—although Methany had handled the press quite coolly at the just finished ceremony, despite a wild scene of flash bulbs, whirring cameras, importunate questioners from the world press. We noted that the US government obviously preferred that the men take a military plane, yet had assured us at least twice that the fliers were free to choose their own route home.

On the side of a commercial flight was only one factor: the North Vietnamese had indicated to Dan Berrigan and me (without setting it as a condition for the release) that they would not be pleased if the fliers were immediately trundled into a military plane and taken to a military base. Somehow, they thought that would violate the spirit of the release. It was not that they had illusions about the men rejecting military life after their arrival in the States; indeed, they had said to Berrigan and me that it was even conceivable that the three would return to bomb North Vietnam again, and that this would sadden them. But even if this occurred, they said, they would retain their basic feeling that the American people, even the American fighting men, were not their enemies.

After that summary of the alternatives, Major Overly spoke very firmly: "Our first concern must be for the fellow prisoners we left behind, and the possibility of future releases by the North Vietnamese. It's clear that we should go back to the States together by commercial flight." The other two agreed immediately.

The flight from Hanoi to Vientiane was smooth; the stewardess served candies and aperitifs and we all relaxed. I sat between Major Overly and Captain Black. Father Berrigan sat with Methany. Overly told me about his experiences in captivity. "I was shot down north of the DMZ. The next twenty-eight days—the trek, under military guard, north to Hanoi—were an experience I never want to have again. I was abused, spat on, threatened, beaten. But I could understand exactly why those people would want to kill me. My guard saved my life three times. It was all strange. One moment, someone would want to kill me. The next minute another Vietnamese would act toward me with such compassion that it just staggered me. I had a huge infection on my back and was in great pain. They gave me sulfa, and after a long time it was cured. When I got to the regular prison, the worst was over. We were well treated. I got no indoctrination, just a few books on Vietnamese history. We got plenty to eat, medical care as needed. The Air Force has a rule against men shot down returning to the combat zone; that's fine with me. I've got three years to go before I can retire. I'd like to do something State-side maybe."

Overly and Black knew I had written some books; they wondered how they could get copies. I promised to send them some, took their addresses. Overly said: "Before this trip is over, I'm going to tell you my whole story, in detail. I think we owe that much to you fellows."

That never happened. As we taxied into the Vientiane airfield, the pilot relayed a message from the tower: "Will the five men connected with the prisoner release please remain aboard the plane while the other passengers descend?" We could see a great gathering on the field of newsmen, cameras, lights. The other passengers got off. Four neatly dressed men got on, and introduced themselves. One was the American Ambassador to Laos, William Sullivan. The others were his air attaché, his naval attaché, his press attaché. Sullivan asked the fliers if they needed medical attention. (His whole manner was crisp, neat, cool toward the three; but perhaps Berrigan and I could not understand the sentiment that lies beneath official exteriors—did not McNamara choke up when saying good-by to the Pentagon?) They said no, they had no urgent medical problems. (One of the statements made later by a navy spokesman was that the men took military planes so they could have medical attention. We have developed the technology of the lie far beyond the crude days of the Commandments.)

Sullivan moved quickly to his most important business: "You

men can choose whether you go home by commercial line or by military plane. However, you do understand that you are still members of the armed forces, and it is my duty to report to you that the Department of Defense has expressed the preference that you go home by military aircraft. About 100 feet away on this airfield is an army jet, waiting and ready to take the three of you to Udorn Airfield in Thailand, and then tomorrow you will fly home. I might add that this decision was made in Washington." He hesitated just a moment. "Indeed, it comes from the White House."

There was a bit of silence. Then Major Overly responded. "Sir, I have been in the Air Force seventeen years, and when my government speaks like that, I know what it means. We will go back by military aircraft." Captain Black quickly assented. Lieutenant Methany was obviously upset. He said: "Wait a minute. Let's talk about this." Then followed forty minutes of tense argument in the confines of the old Boeing plane. We agreed on the advantages of the military plane (speed, less harassment by the press), but asked if this overrode the matter of future prisoner releases by the North Vietnamese. Whether or not the Vietnamese released future prisoners, the Ambassador said, was a cold matter of political calculation with them. (In the grade-B movies about the Red Menace, the thickset man with the heavy Russian accent says: "There is no room for sentiment in our considerations, comrades." We have not yet done justice in grade-A movies to the same point made by slim, dapper men, speaking in our own clear tongue.)

The ambassador turned to me: "I didn't know the North Vietnamese were setting conditions for this release." They were not setting conditions, I replied; it was a more subtle problem, one of psychology and spirit. The ambassador questioned how we knew this was indeed what the North Vietnamese preferred. Major Overly cut in: "The North Vietnamese told us exactly the same thing." (This was news to me; I had not known that they expressed their feelings also to the fliers.)

What advantage of the military plane, we persisted, could be more important than the question of future prisoner releases? Well, the ambassador countered, it might be hurtful to such releases if the men met the press and said the wrong things. We told about the very first press encounter in Hanoi, where the fliers had handled themselves admirably, with no embarrassment to anyone. Besides, the simple device of a prepared statement could take care of such problems. So, what other objection was there?

The ambassador could only keep saying: "They have considered all the alternatives in Washington before making their decision. The best minds in Washington have been involved." (We let this slide; the NLF offensive was still going on, so why rub it in about the "best minds"?) We did suggest that the men in Washington, smart as they were, had not been recently in North Vietnam, had not spoken with North Vietnamese, were hardly in a position to judge this specific situation as well as the fliers or us. Sullivan's reply, a stunning *non sequitur*, was a good example of how an intelligent man, trapped in a bureaucratic decision, makes unintelligent statements: "The man in Washington who had much to do with this decision came out of a Japanese prison camp in 1945 weighing 97 pounds."

Berrigan had had enough. "Let's go," he said to me. The fliers were very troubled. Methany was fighting back some indefinable emotion. They shook our hands. "We're sorry," they kept repeating. "Good luck," we said. Overly whispered something to me, quite warm, quite personal. They walked out, talked to the cameras, lights, crowding newsmen, then went to the army jet. They were no longer prisoners, yet not quite free.

As I write this, two weeks later, that argument about the route home seems as it did at the start of our trip, ludicrously trivial; an almost childish dispute on both sides. Three men released from war—how puny a fact was even that, with millions still trapped in the caldron of death that is Vietnam. Why should these be released, these who dutifully bombed villages, roads, people, schools (not deliberately, let's agree—only inevitably)? Why not the three tiny Vietnamese kids we found one day squatting in the entrance to the air-raid shelter? Perhaps there was a larger issue involved. Perhaps we move closer to the end of the war whenever even one of the parties shows compassion, in a unilateral act, and toward the most guilty of warriors—the blind bombardiers.

Now don't get sentimental, even my most radical friends insist; there must have been *some* political motive on the part of the North Vietnamese in this prisoner release. Well, all right. But all decent acts in this world are marred to some degree by selfish motivation; if we let that fact determine how we respond to such acts, the possibility of ending the vicious cycle of reciprocal cruelty is foreclosed. If people and nations can react only on the basis of the most cynical interpretations of the other party's conduct, the world doesn't have much of a chance.

There is something else. I asked Oanh that last day (as we sat next to each other at a little goodbye luncheon) if there wasn't *something* we should ask from the US government in return for the release. He shook his head. "You don't understand. We have released these men in the time of our lunar New Year. That is a very important holiday to us, very deep in our tradition. It is the time when, wherever we are, we return to our families for the New Year. So, we thought of a small gesture, even in the midst of war, in the spirit of the holiday: to release three men to go back to their families." And so they preferred that the fliers return directly to their homes, rather than what did take place: the immediate flight of the pilots to the very air base in Thailand from which one of the men (Black) had taken off to bomb North Vietnam.

Against the cynicism of the Ambassador (as well as my own) another fact must be measured: it is canonized in the revolutionary ideology of North Vietnam that enemy soldiers are to be treated with compassion. From the start of the war against the French, Ho Chi Minh insisted on this. In a message (September 26, 1945) meant not for the world but for his own troops, he said: "I want to recommend to our Southern compatriots just one thing: as far as the Frenchmen captured in the war are concerned, we must watch them carefully, but we must also treat them generously. We must show to the world, and to the French people in particular, that we want only independence and freedom, that we are not struggling for the sake of individual enmity and rancor. We must show to the world that we are an intelligent people, more civilized than the homicidal invaders."

The word Ho used was "show," not "tell." If the prisoner release was "propaganda" (as newspaper men kept saying, before and after our flight to Hanoi) it was propaganda by *deed*, which, if generally adopted, would improve the world overnight. The United States, if envious, could respond with its own propaganda move: stop the bombing in the North. Or with the greatest propaganda of all: withdrawing all its bombers, all its guns and troops, from Vietnam.

The pinched, mean reaction to the prisoner release (a "propaganda ploy," *Life* said lifelessly) is an indicator of what has happened to the spirit of generosity we always liked to believe was characteristic of America. Some future generation will catch the irony better: that a tiny country, under daily attack, should deliver back to the behemoth three of its marauders. And the behemoth, meanwhile, seeks to imprison five men who have not bombed or killed a single soul—but who have spoken the forbidden words to the behemoth's children: Thou Shalt Not Kill.

Whatever softening possibility came from that small act of the Vietnamese was destroyed by this country's fear. Never in history has a country been so rich, so powerful, and so fearful. In this case, it was a fear of something as small as three very straight American airmen saying something that would slightly embarrass Washington—an event so unlikely, and so minor if it did occur, that only a government almost hysterical in its anxiety would behave as ours did. True, a government so harassed by fact as ours today, so trembling on the brink, fears even the slightest nudge, the smallest breeze from an unexpected direction. It refuses to take even the tiniest of risks.

In risk, however, lies the only hope of escape from deep troubles—the risk of humane response to humane acts, or even the risk of unilateral initiatives. This is not possible, however, when a nation has forgotten its professed values and is instead obsessed with political advantage as an ultimate objective, when it has adopted as a universal criterion for all its actions that of Colonel Cathcart in *Catch-22*, who measured everything in the world by a simple test: "Will it give me a black eye, or put a feather in my cap?" Our sickness is even worse than that, because our single test is (and we are ready to blow up the world on the results): Will it give *them* a black eye, or a feather in their cap?

This obsessive fear, that if the next point is won or lost, the game, the world, and all the galaxies are lost (those deadly dominoes again), leads to disregard not only of the lives of the enemy's children but of one's own. When the American people discover this—that our government is not only indifferent to whether the Vietnamese live or die but also to whether Americans live or die— then we shall have a great commotion through the land, and the war will come to a grinding halt. ✱

A PEOPLE'S CONSTITUTION:
SOME TRUTHS ARE NOT SELF-EVIDENT

AUGUST 1, 1987

This year Americans are talking about the Constitution but asking the wrong questions, such as, Could the Founding Fathers have done better? That concern is pointless, 200 years after the fact. Or, Does the Constitution provide the framework for a just and democratic society today? That question is also misplaced, because the Constitution, whatever its language and however interpreted by the Supreme Court, does not determine the degree of justice, liberty or democracy in our society.

The proper question, I believe, is not how good a document is or was the Constitution but, What effect does it have on the quality of our lives? And the answer to that, it seems to me, is,

Very little. The Constitution makes promises it cannot by itself keep, and therefore deludes us into complacency about the rights we have. It is conspicuously silent on certain other rights that all human beings deserve. And it pretends to set limits on government powers, when in fact those limits are easily ignored.

I am not arguing that the Constitution has no importance; words have moral power and principles can be useful even when ambiguous. But, like other historic documents, the Constitution is of minor importance compared with the actions that citizens take, especially when those actions are joined in social movements. Such movements have worked, historically, to secure the rights our human sensibilities tell us are self-evidently ours, whether or not those rights are "granted" by the Constitution.

Let me illustrate my point with five issues of liberty and justice:

§ First is the matter of racial equality. When slavery was abolished, it was not by constitutional fiat but by the joining of military necessity with the moral force of a great antislavery movement, acting outside the Constitution and often against the law. The Thirteenth, Fourteenth and Fifteenth Amendments wrote into the Constitution rights that extralegal action had already won. But the Fourteenth and Fifteenth Amendments were ignored for almost a hundred years. The right to equal protection of the law and the right to vote, even the Supreme Court decision in *Brown v. Board of Education* in 1954 underlining the meaning of the equal protection clause, did not become operative until blacks, in the fifteen years following the Montgomery bus boycott, shook up the nation by tumultuous actions inside and outside the law.

The Constitution played a helpful but marginal role in all that. Black people, in the political context of the 1960s, would have demanded equality whether or not the Constitution called for it, just as the antislavery movement demanded abolition even in the absence of constitutional support.

§ What about the most vaunted of constitutional rights, free speech? Historically, the Supreme Court has given the right to free speech only shaky support, seesawing erratically by sometimes affirming and sometimes overriding restrictions. Whatever a distant Court decided, the real right of citizens to free expression has been determined by the immediate power of the local police on the street, by the employer in the workplace and by the financial limits on the ability to use the mass media.

The existence of a First Amendment has been inspirational but its protection elusive. Its reality has depended on the willingness of citizens, whether labor organizers, socialists or Jehovah's Witnesses, to insist on their right to speak and write. Liberties have not been given; they have been taken. And whether in the future we have a right to say what we want, or air what we say, will be determined not by the existence of the First Amendment or the latest Supreme Court decision but by whether we are courageous enough to speak up at the risk of being jailed or fired, organized enough to defend our speech against official interference and can command resources enough to get our ideas before a reasonably large public.

§ What of economic justice? The Constitution is silent on the right to earn a moderate income, silent on the rights to medical care and decent housing as legitimate claims of every human being from infancy to old age. Whatever degree of economic justice has been attained in this country (impressive compared with others, shameful compared with our resources) cannot be attributed to something in the Constitution. It is the result of the concerted action of laborers and farmers over the centuries—using strikes, boycotts and minor rebellions of all sorts—to get redress of grievances directly from employers and indirectly from legislators. In the future, as in the past, the Constitution will sleep as citizens battle over the distribution of the nation's wealth, and will be awakened only to mark the score.

§ On sexual equality the Constitution is also silent. What women have achieved thus far is the result of their own determination, in the feminist upsurge of the nineteenth and early twentieth centuries, and the more recent women's liberation movement. Women have accomplished this outside the Constitution, by raising female and male consciousness and inducing courts and legislators to *recognize* what the Constitution ignores.

§ Finally, in an age in which war approaches genocide, the irrelevance of the Constitution is especially striking. Long, ravaging conflicts in Korea and Vietnam were waged without following constitutional procedures, and if there is a nuclear exchange, the decision to launch US missiles will be made, as it was in those cases, by the President and a few advisers. The public will be shut out of the process and deliberately kept uninformed by an intricate web of secrecy and deceit. The current Iran/*contra* scandal hearings before Congressional select committees should be understood as exposing not an aberration but a steady state of foreign policy.

It was not constitutional checks and balances but an aroused populace that prodded Lyndon Johnson and then Richard Nixon into deciding to extricate the United States from Vietnam. In the immediate future, our lives will depend not on the existence of the Constitution but on the power of an aroused citizenry demanding that we not go to war, and on Americans refusing, as did so many GIs and civilians in the Vietnam era, to cooperate in the conduct of a war.

The Constitution, like the Bible, has some good words. It is also, like the Bible, easily manipulated, distorted, ignored and used to make us feel comfortable and protected. But we risk the loss of our lives and liberties if we depend on a mere document to defend them. A constitution is a fine adornment for a democratic society, but it is no substitute for the energy, boldness and concerted action of the citizens. ✳

THE OTHERS

FEBRUARY 11, 2002

E very day for several months, *The New York Times* did what should always be done when a tragedy is summed up in a statistic: It gave us miniature portraits of the human beings who died on September 11—their names, photos, glimmers of their personalities, their idiosyncrasies, how friends and loved ones remember them.

As the director of the New-York Historical Society said: "The peculiar genius of it was to put a human face on numbers that are unimaginable to most of us.... It's so obvious that every one of them was a person who deserved to live a full and successful and happy life. You see what was lost."

I was deeply moved, reading those intimate sketches—"A Poet of Bensonhurst... A Friend, A Sister... Someone to Lean On... Laughter, Win or Lose." I thought: Those who celebrated the grisly deaths of the people in the twin towers and the Pentagon as a blow to symbols of American dominance in the world—what if, instead of symbols, they could see, up close, the faces of those who lost their lives? I wonder if they would have second thoughts, second feelings.

Then it occurred to me: What if all those Americans who declare their support for Bush's "war on terror" could see, instead of those elusive symbols—Osama bin Laden, Al Qaeda—the real human beings who have died under our bombs? I do believe they would have second thoughts.

There are those on the left, normally compassionate people whose instincts go against war, who were, surprisingly, seduced by early Administration assurances and consoled themselves with words like "limited" military action and "measured" response. I think they, too, if confronted with the magnitude of the human suffering caused by the war in Afghanistan, would have second thoughts.

True, there are those in Washington and around the country who would not be moved, who are eager—like their counterparts elsewhere in the world—to kill for some cause. But most Americans would begin to understand that we have been waging a war on ordinary men, women and children. And that these human beings have died because they happened to live in Afghan villages in the vicinity of vaguely defined "military targets," and that the bombing that destroyed their lives is in no way a war on terrorism, because it has no chance of ending terrorism and is itself a form of terrorism.

But how can this be done—this turning of ciphers into human beings? In contrast with the vignettes about the the victims featured in the *Times*, there are few available details about the dead men, women and children in Afghanistan.

We would need to study the scattered news reports, usually in the inside sections of the *Times* and the *Washington Post*, but also in the international press—Reuters; the London *Times*, *Guardian* and *Independent*; and Agence France-Presse.

These reports have been mostly out of sight of the general public (indeed, virtually never reported on national television, where most Americans get their news), and so dispersed as to reinforce the idea that the bombing of civilians has been an infrequent event, a freak accident, an unfortunate mistake.

Listen to the language of the Pentagon: "We cannot confirm the report... civilian casualties are inevitable... we don't know if they were our weapons... it was an accident... incorrect coordinates had been entered... they are deliberately putting civilians in our bombing targets... the village was a legitimate military target... it just didn't happen... we regret any loss of civilian life."

"Collateral damage," Timothy McVeigh said, using a Pentagon expression, when asked about the children who died when he bombed the federal building in Oklahoma City. After reports of the bombing of one village, Pentagon spokeswoman Victoria Clarke said, "We take extraordinary care…. There is unintended damage. There is collateral damage. Thus far, it has been extremely limited." The Agence France-Presse reporter quoting her said: "Refugees arriving in Pakistan suggested otherwise. Several recounted how twenty people, including nine children, had been killed as they tried to flee an attack on the southern Afghan town of Tirin Kot."

Listening to the repeated excuses given by Bush, Rumsfeld and others, one recalls Colin Powell's reply at the end of the Gulf War, when questioned about Iraqi casualties: "That is really not a matter I am terribly interested in." If, indeed, a strict definition of the word "deliberate" does not apply to the bombs dropped on the civilians of Afghanistan, then we can offer, thinking back to Powell's statement, an alternate characterization: "a reckless disregard for human life."

The denials of the Pentagon are uttered confidently half a world away in Washington. But there are on-the-spot press reports from the villages, from hospitals where the wounded lie and from the Pakistan border, where refugees have fled the bombs. If we put these reports together, we get brief glimpses of the human tragedies in Afghanistan—the names of the dead, the villages that were bombed, the words of a father who lost his children, the ages of the children. We would then have to multiply these stories by the hundreds, think of the unreported incidents and know that the numbers go into the thousands. A professor of economics at the University of New Hampshire, Marc Herold, has done a far more thorough survey of the press than I have. He lists location, type of weapon used and sources of information. He finds the civilian death toll in Afghanistan up to December 10 exceeding 3,500 (he has since raised the figure to 4,000), a sad and startling parallel to the number of victims in the twin towers.

The New York Times was able to interrogate friends and family of the New York dead, but for the Afghans, we will have to imagine the hopes and dreams of those who died, especially the children, for whom forty or fifty years of mornings, love, friendship, sunsets and the sheer exhilaration of being alive were extinguished by monstrous machines sent over their land by men far away.

My intention is not at all to diminish our compassion for the victims of the terrorism of September 11, but to enlarge that compassion to include the victims of all terrorism, in any place, at any time, whether perpetrated by Middle East fanatics or American politicians.

In that spirit, I present the following news items (only a fraction of those in my files), hoping that there is the patience to go through them, like the patience required to read the portraits of the September 11 dead, like the patience required to read the 58,000 names on the Vietnam Memorial:

From a hospital in Jalalabad, Afghanistan, reported in the *Boston Globe* by John Donnelly on December 5:

"In one bed lay Noor Mohammad, 10, who was a bundle of bandages. He lost his eyes and hands to the bomb that hit his house after Sunday dinner. Hospital director Guloja Shimwari shook his head at the boy's wounds. 'The United States must be thinking he is Osama,' Shimwari said. 'If he is not Osama, then why would they do this?'"

The report continued:

"The hospital's morgue received 17 bodies last weekend, and officials here estimate at least 89 civilians were killed in several villages. In the hospital yesterday, a bomb's damage could be chronicled in the life of one family. A bomb had killed the father, Faisal Karim. In one bed was his wife, Mustafa Jama, who had severe head injuries.... Around her, six of her children were in bandages.... One of them, Zahidullah, 8, lay in a coma."

In *The New York Times*, Barry Bearak, reporting December 15 from the village of Madoo, Afghanistan, tells of the destruction of fifteen houses and their occupants. "'In the night, as we slept, they dropped the bombs on us,' said Paira Gul, a young man whose eyes were aflame with bitterness. His sisters and their families had perished, he said.... The houses were small, the bombing precise. No structure escaped the thundering havoc. Fifteen houses, 15 ruins.... 'Most of the dead are children,' Tor Tul said."

Another *Times* reporter, C.J. Chivers, writing from the village of Charykari on December 12, reported "a terrifying and rolling barrage that the villagers believe was the payload of an American B-52.... The villagers say 30 people died.... One man, Muhibullah, 40, led the way through his yard and showed three unexploded cluster bombs he is afraid to touch. A fourth was not a dud. It landed near his porch. 'My son was sitting there...the metal went inside him.' The boy, Zumarai, 5, is in a hospital in Kunduz, with wounds to leg and abdomen. His sister, Sharpari, 10, was killed. 'The United States killed my daughter and injured my son,' Mr. Muhibullah said. 'Six of my cows were destroyed and all of my wheat and rice was burned. I am very angry. I miss my daughter.'"

From the *Washington Post*, October 24, from Peshawar, Pakistan, by Pamela Constable: "Sardar, a taxi driver and father of 12, said his family had spent night after night listening to the bombing in their community south of Kabul. One night during the first week, he said, a bomb aimed at a nearby radio station struck a house, killing all five members of the family living there. 'There was no sign of a home left,' he said. 'We just collected the pieces of bodies and buried them.'"

Reporter Catherine Philp of the *Times* of London, reporting October 25 from Quetta, Pakistan: "It was not long after 7 pm on Sunday when the bombs began to fall over the outskirts of Torai village.... Rushing outside, Mauroof saw a massive fireball. Morning brought an end to the bombing and...a neighbor arrived to tell him that some 20 villagers had been killed in the blasts, among them ten of his relatives. 'I saw the body of one of my brothers-in-law being pulled from the debris,' Mauroof said. 'The lower part of his body had been blown away. Some of the other bodies were unrecognizable. There were heads missing and arms blown off.' The roll call of the dead read like an invitation list to a family wedding: his mother-in-law, two sisters-in-law, three brothers-in-law, and four of his sister's five young children, two girls and two boys, all under the age of eight."

Human Rights Watch report, October 26: "25-year-old Sami-ullah...rushed home to rescue his family...he found the bodies of his 20-year-old wife and three of his children: Mohibullah, aged six; Harifullah, aged three; and Bibi Aysha, aged one.... Also killed were his two brothers, Nasiullah, aged eight, and Ghaziullah, aged six, as well as two of his sisters, aged fourteen and eleven."

From Reuters, October 28, Sayed Salahuddin reporting from Kabul: "A US bomb flattened a flimsy mud-brick home in Kabul Sunday, blowing apart seven children as they ate breakfast with their father.... Sobs racked the body of a middle-aged man as he cradled the head of his baby, its dust-covered body dressed only in a blue diaper, lying beside the bodies of three other children, their colorful clothes layered with debris from their shattered homes."

Washington Post Foreign Service, November 2, from Quetta, Pakistan, by Rajiv Chandrasekaran: "The thunder of the first explosions jolted Nasir Ahmed awake.... He grabbed his 14-year-old niece and scurried into a communal courtyard. From there, he said, they watched as civilians who survived the bombing run, including his niece and a woman holding her 5-year-old son, were gunned down by a slow-moving, propeller-driven aircraft circling overheard. When the gunship departed an hour later, at least 25 people in the village—all civilians—were dead, according to accounts of the incident provided today by Ahmed, two other witnesses, and several relatives of people in the village.

"The Pentagon confirmed that the village was hit...but officials said they believe the aircraft struck a legitimate military target.... Asked about civilian casualties, the official said, 'We don't know. We're not on the ground.'

"Shaida, 14... 'Americans are not good.... They killed my mother. They killed my father. I don't understand why.'"

A *Newsday* report on November 24 from Kabul, by James Rupert: "In the sprawling, mud-brick slum of Qala-ye-Khatir, most men were kneeling in the mosques at morning prayer on November 6 when a quarter-ton of steel and high explosives hurtled from the sky into the home of Gul Ahmed, a carpet weaver. The American bomb detonated, killing Ahmed, his five daughters, one of his wives, and a son. Next door, it demolished the home of Sahib Dad and killed two of his children.

"Ross Chamberlain, the coordinator for UN mine-clearing operations in much of Afghanistan.... 'There's really no such thing as a precision bombing.... We are finding more cases of errant targeting than accurate targeting, more misses than hits.'"

The New York Times, November 22, from Ghaleh Shafer, Afghanistan: "10-year-old Mohebolah Seraj went out to collect wood for his family, and thought he had happened upon a food packet. He picked it up and lost three fingers in an explosion. Doctors say he will probably lose his whole hand...his mother, Sardar Seraj...said that she cried and told the doctors not to cut off her son's whole hand.

"The hospital where her son is being cared for is a grim place, lacking power and basic sanitation. In one room lay Muhammad

Ayoub, a 20-year-old who was in the house when the cluster bomb initially landed. He lost a leg and his eyesight, and his face was severely disfigured. He moaned in agony.... Hospital officials said that a 16-year-old had been decapitated."

A *New York Times* report on December 3 from Jalalabad, Afghanistan, by Tim Weiner: "The commanders, who are pro-American...say that four nearby villages were struck this weekend, leaving 80 or more people dead and others wounded.... The villages are near Tora Bora, the mountain camp where Mr. bin Laden is presumed to be hiding. A Pentagon spokesman said Saturday that the bombing of civilians near Tora Bora 'never happened.'

"Eight men guarding the building [a district office building]...were killed, [*mujahedeen* commander] Hajji Zaman said. He gave the names of the dead as Zia ul-Hassan, 16; Wilayat Khan, 17; Abdul Wadi, 20; Jany, 22; Abdul Wahid, 30; Hajji Wazir, 35; Hajji Nasser, also 35; and Awlia Gul, 37...Ali Shah, 26, of Landa Khel, said, 'There is no one in this village who is part of Al Qaeda.'

"Witnesses said that at least 50 and as many as 200 villagers had been killed.

"'We are poor people,' [Muhammad] Tahir said. 'Our trees are our only shelter from the cold and wind. The trees have been bombed. Our waterfall, our only source of water—they bombed it. Where is the humanity?'"

The *Independent*, December 4: "The village where nothing happened.... The cemetery on the hill contains 40 freshly dug graves, unmarked and identical. And the village of Kama Ado has ceased to exist.... And all this is very strange because, on Saturday morning—when American B-52s unloaded dozens of bombs that killed 115 men, women and children—nothing happened.... We know this because the US Department of Defence told us so.... 'It just didn't happen.'"

The New York Times, December 12, David Rohde, writing from Ghazni, Afghanistan: "Each ward of the Ghazni Hospital features a new calamity. In the first, two 14-year-old boys had lost parts of their hands when they picked up land mines. 'I was playing with a toy and it exploded' said one of them, Muhammad Allah.... A woman named Rose lay on a bed in the corner of the room, grunting with each breath. Her waiflike children slept nearby, whimpering periodically. Early on Sunday morning, shrapnel from an American bomb tore through the woman's abdomen, broke her 4-year-old son's leg and ripped into her 6-year-old daughter's head, doctors here said. A second 6-year-old girl in the room was paralyzed from the waist down. X-rays showed how a tiny shard of metal had neatly severed her spinal cord."

Reported in the *Chicago Tribune*, December 28, by Paul Salopek, from Madoo, Afghanistan: "'American soldiers came after the bombing and asked if any Al Qaeda had lived here,' said villager Paira Gul. 'Is that an Al Qaeda?' Gul asked, pointing to a child's severed foot he had excavated minutes earlier from a smashed house. 'Tell me' he said, his voice choking with fury, 'is that what an Al Qaeda looks like?'"

Reuters, December 31, from Qalaye Niazi, Afghanistan:

"Janat Gul said 24 members of his family were killed in the pre-dawn US bombing raid on Qalaye Niazi, and described himself as the sole survivor.... In the US Major Pete Mitchell—a spokesman for US Central Command—said: 'We are aware of the incident and we are currently investigating.'"

Yes, these reports appeared, but scattered through the months of bombing and on the inside pages, or buried in larger stories and accompanied by solemn government denials. With no access to alternative information, it is not surprising that a majority of Americans have approved of what they have been led to think is a "war on terror."

Recall that Americans at first supported the war in Vietnam. But once the statistics of the dead became visible human beings—once they saw not only the body bags of young GIs piling up by the tens of thousands but also the images of the napalmed children, the burning huts, the massacred families at My Lai—shock and indignation fueled a national movement to end the war.

I do believe that if people could see the consequences of the bombing campaign as vividly as we were all confronted with the horrifying photos in the wake of September 11, if they saw on television night after night the blinded and maimed children, the weeping parents of Afghanistan, they might ask: Is this the way to combat terrorism?

Surely it is time, half a century after Hiroshima, to embrace a universal morality, to think of all children, everywhere, as our own. ✳

HOW TO GET OUT OF IRAQ

MAY 24, 2004

Contribution to a forum

Any "practical" approach to the situation in Iraq, any prescription for what to do now, must start with the understanding that the present US military occupation is morally unacceptable. Amnesty International, a year after the invasion, reported: "Scores of unarmed people have been killed due to excessive or unnecessary use of lethal force by coalition forces during public demonstrations, at checkpoints and in house raids. Thousands of people have been detained [estimates range from 8,500 to 15,000, often under harsh conditions] and subjected to prolonged and often unacknowledged detention. Many have been tortured or ill-treated and some have died in custody." The prospect, if the occupation continues, whether by the United States or by an international force (as John Kerry seems to be proposing), is of continued suffering and death for both Iraqis and Americans.

The history of military occupations of Third World countries is that they bring neither democracy nor security. The laments that "we mustn't cut and run," "we must stay the course," our "reputation" will be imperiled, etc., are exactly what we heard when at the start of the Vietnam escalation some of us called for immediate withdrawal. The result of staying the course was 58,000 Americans and several million Vietnamese dead.

The only rational argument for continuing on the present course is that things will be worse if we leave. In Vietnam, they promised a bloodbath if we left. That did not happen. It was said that if we did not drop the bomb on Hiroshima, we would have to invade Japan and huge casualties would follow. We know now and knew then that this was not true. The truth is, no one knows what will happen if the United States withdraws. We face a choice between the certainty of mayhem if we stay, and the uncertainty of what will follow if we leave.

What would be a reasonably good scenario to accompany our departure? The UN should arrange, as US forces leave, for an international group of peacekeepers and negotiators from the Arab countries to bring together Shiites, Sunnis and Kurds, and work out a solution for self-governance that would give all three groups a share in political power. Simultaneously, the UN should arrange for shipments of food and medicine, from the United States and other countries, as well as engineers to help rebuild the country.

The one thing to be avoided is for the United States, which destroyed Iraq and caused perhaps a million deaths through two invasions and ten years of sanctions, to play any leading role in the future of that country. In that case, terrorism would surely flourish. It is for the United States to withdraw from Iraq. It is for the international community, particularly the Arab world, to try to reconstruct a nation at peace. That gives the Iraqi people a chance. Continued US occupation gives them no chance. *

BEYOND THE NEW DEAL

APRIL 7, 2008

e might wonder why no Democratic Party contender for the presidency has invoked the memory of the New Deal and its unprecedented series of laws aimed at helping people in need. The New Deal was tentative, cautious, bold enough to shake the pillars of the system but not to replace them. It created many jobs but left 9 million unemployed. It built public housing but not nearly enough. It helped large commercial farmers but not tenant farmers. Excluded from its programs were the poorest of the poor, especially blacks. As farm laborers, migrants or domestic workers, they didn't qualify for unemployment insurance, a minimum wage, Social Security or farm subsidies.

Still, in today's climate of endless war and uncontrolled greed, drawing upon the heritage of the 1930s would be a huge step forward. Perhaps the momentum of such a project could carry the nation past the limits of FDR's reforms, especially if there were a popular upsurge that demanded it. A candidate who points to the New Deal as a model for innovative legislation would be drawing on the huge reputation Franklin Roosevelt and his policies enjoy in this country, an admiration matched by no President since Lincoln. Imagine the response a Democratic candidate would get from the electorate if he or she spoke as follows:

"Our nation is in crisis, just as it was when Roosevelt took office. At that time, people desperately needed help, they needed jobs, decent housing, protection in old age. They needed to know that the government was for them and not just for the wealthy classes. This is what the American people need today.

"I will do what the New Deal did, to make up for the failure of the market system. It put millions of people to work through the Works Progress Administration, at all kinds of jobs, from building schools, hospitals, playgrounds, to repairing streets and bridges, to writing symphonies and painting murals and putting on plays. We can do that today for workers displaced by closed factories, for professionals downsized by a failed economy, for families needing two or three incomes to survive, for writers and musicians and other artists who struggle for security.

"The New Deal's Civilian Conservation Corps at its peak employed 500,000 young people. They lived in camps, planted millions of trees, reclaimed millions of acres of land, built 97,000 miles of fire roads, protected natural habitats, restocked fish and gave emergency help to people threatened by floods.

"We can do that today, by bringing our soldiers home from war and from the military bases we have in 130 countries. We will recruit young people not to fight but to clean up our lakes and rivers, build homes for people in need, make our cities beautiful, be ready to help with disasters like Katrina. The military is having a hard time recruiting young men and women for war, and with good reason. We will have no such problem enlisting the young to build rather than destroy.

"We can learn from the Social Security program and the GI Bill of Rights, which were efficient government programs, doing for older people and for veterans what private enterprise could not do. We can go beyond the New Deal, extending the principle of social security to health security with a totally free government-run health system. We can extend the GI Bill of Rights to a Civilian Bill of Rights, offering free higher education for all.

"We will have trillions of dollars to pay for these programs if we do two things: if we concentrate our taxes on the richest 1 percent of the population, not only their incomes but their accumulated wealth, and if we downsize our gigantic military machine, declaring ourselves a peaceful nation.

"We will not pay attention to those who complain that this is 'big government.' We have seen big government used for war and to give benefits to the wealthy. We will use big government for the people."

How refreshing it would be if a presidential candidate reminded us of the experience of the New Deal and defied the corporate elite as Roosevelt did, on the eve of his 1936 re-election. Referring to the determination of the wealthy classes to defeat him, he told a huge crowd at Madison Square Garden: "They are unanimous in their hatred for me—and I welcome their hatred." I believe that a candidate who showed such boldness would win a smashing victory at the polls.

The innovations of the New Deal were fueled by the militant demands for change that swept the country as FDR began his presidency: the tenants' groups; the Unemployed Councils; the millions on strike on the West Coast, in the Midwest and the South; the disruptive actions of desperate people seeking food, housing, jobs—the turmoil threatening the foundations of American capitalism. We will need a similar mobilization of citizens today, to unmoor from corporate control whoever becomes President. To match the New Deal, to go beyond it, is an idea whose time has come. ✳

A Big Government Bailout

OCTOBER 27, 2008

I t is sad to see both major parties agree to spend $700 billion of taxpayer money to bail out huge financial institutions that are notable for two characteristics: incompetence and greed. There is a much better solution to the financial crisis. But it would require discarding what has been conventional wisdom for too long: that government intervention in the economy ("big government") must be avoided like the plague, because the "free market" can be depended on to guide the economy toward growth and justice. Surely the sight of Wall Street begging for government aid is almost comic in light of its long devotion to a "free market" unregulated by government.

Let's face a historical truth: We have never had a free market.

We have always had government intervention in the economy, and indeed that intervention has been welcomed by the captains of finance and industry. These titans of wealth hypocritically warned against "big government" but only when government threatened to regulate their activities or when it contemplated passing some of the nation's wealth on to the neediest people. They had no quarrel with big government when it served their needs.

It started way back when the Founding Fathers met in Philadelphia in 1787 to draft the Constitution. The year before, they had seen armed rebellions of farmers in western Massachusetts (Shays's Rebellion), where farms were being seized for nonpayment of taxes. Thousands of farmers surrounded the courthouses and refused to allow their farms to be auctioned off. The Founders' correspondence at this time makes clear their worries about such uprisings getting out of hand. Gen. Henry Knox wrote to George Washington, warning that the ordinary soldier who fought in the Revolution thought that by contributing to the defeat of England he deserved an equal share of the wealth of the country, that "the property of the United States…ought to be the common property of all."

In framing the Constitution, the Founders created "big government" powerful enough to put down the rebellions of farmers, to return escaped slaves to their masters and to put down Indian resistance when settlers moved westward. The first big bailout was the decision of the new government to redeem for full value the almost worthless bonds held by speculators.

From the start, in the first sessions of the first Congress, the government interfered with the free market by establishing tariffs to subsidize manufacturers and by becoming a partner with private banks in establishing a national bank. This role of big government supporting the interests of the business classes has continued all through the nation's history. Thus, in the nineteenth century the government subsidized canals and the merchant marine. In the decades before and during the Civil War, the government gave away some 100 million acres of land to the railroads, along with considerable loans to keep the railroad interests in business. The 10,000 Chinese and 3,000 Irish who worked on the transcontinental railroad got no free land and no loans, only long hours, little pay, accidents and sickness.

The principle of government helping big business and refusing government largesse to the poor was bipartisan, upheld by Republicans and Democrats. President Grover Cleveland, a Democrat, vetoed a bill to give $10,000 to Texas farmers to help them buy seed grain during a drought, saying, "Federal aid in such cases encourages the expectation of paternal care on the part of the government and weakens the sturdiness of our national character." But that same year, he used the gold surplus to pay wealthy bondholders $28 above the value of each bond—a gift of $5 million.

Cleveland was enunciating the principle of rugged individualism—that we must make our fortunes on our own, without help from the government. In his 1931 *Harper's* essay "The Myth of Rugged American Individualism," historian Charles Beard carefully cataloged fifteen instances of the government intervening in the economy for the benefit of big business. Beard wrote, "For forty years or more there has not been a President, Republican or Democrat, who has not talked against government interference and then supported measures adding more interference to the huge collection already accumulated."

After World War II the aircraft industry had to be saved by infusions of government money. Then came the oil depletion allowances for the oil companies and the huge bailout for the Chrysler Corporation. In the 1980s the government bailed out the savings and loan industry with hundreds of billions of dollars, and the Cato Institute reports that in 2006 needy corporations like Boeing, Xerox, Motorola, Dow Chemical and General Electric received $92 billion in corporate welfare.

A simple and powerful alternative would be to take that huge sum of money, $700 billion, and give it directly to the people who need it. Let the government declare a moratorium on foreclosures and help homeowners pay off their mortgages. Create a federal jobs program to guarantee work to people who want and need jobs.

We have a historic and successful precedent. The government in the early days of the New Deal put millions of people to work rebuilding the nation's infrastructure. Hundreds of thousands of young people, instead of joining the army to escape poverty, joined the Civil Conservation Corps, which built bridges and highways, cleaned up harbors and rivers. Thousands of artists, musicians and writers were employed by the WPA's arts programs to paint murals, produce plays, write symphonies. The New Deal (defying the cries of "socialism") established Social Security, which, along with the GI Bill, became a model for what government could do to help its people.

That can be carried further, with "health security"—free healthcare for all, administered by the government, paid for from our Treasury, bypassing the insurance companies and the other privateers of the health industry. All that will take more than $700 billion. But the money is there: in the $600 billion for the military budget, once we decide we will not be a warmaking nation anymore, and in the bloated bank accounts of the superrich, once we bring them down to ordinary-rich size by taxing vigorously their income and their wealth.

When the cry goes up, whether from Republicans or Democrats, that this must not be done because it is "big government," the citizens should just laugh. And then agitate and organize on behalf of what the Declaration of Independence promised: that it is the responsibility of government to ensure the equal right of all to "Life, Liberty, and the pursuit of Happiness."

This is a golden opportunity for Obama to distance himself cleanly from McCain as well as the fossilized Democratic Party leaders, giving life to his slogan of change and thereby sweeping into office. And if he doesn't act, it will be up to the people, as it always has been, to raise a shout that will be heard around the world—and compel the politicians to listen. ✳

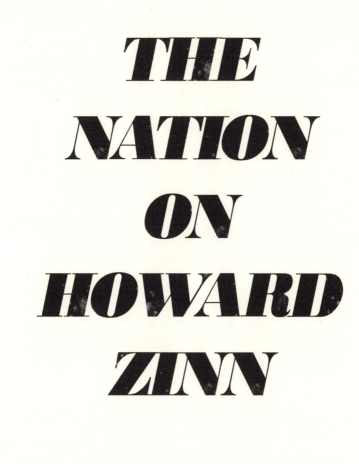

THE
NATION
ON
HOWARD
ZINN

CIVIL DISOBEDIENCE: MORAL OR NOT?

Carl Cohen, December 2, 1968

Review of **Disobedience and Democracy: Nine Fallacies on Law and Order.** Carl Cohen is Professor of Philosophy at University of Michigan, where he has taught since 1955.

ivil disobedience has become one of the most puzzling and provocative issues of the times. There are two kinds of reasons for this. First, those who have recently been engaging in disobedient demonstrations have done so, most usually, to register vehement protest against laws, acts and conditions that cry out for remedy, while remedy continues to elude us. The barbarity of the war in Vieteam; the cruelty of racism at home; the mal-distribution of wealth and power; and, above all, the apparent unwillingness or inability of our national institutions—Congress, the courts, private enterprise—to deal effectively with injustice, frustrate and anger all decent citizens, and force us to ask ourselves how changes we know to be essential can be brought about. Those who practice civil disobedience seek to provide at least a partial answer to this question, often breaking new ground at considerable risk to themselves. Most often we find ourselves in strong sympathy with such disobedients, knowing their intentions honorable and their cause just. Even so, many remain in doubt about the moral justifiability of deliberately unlawful protest. To be sure, the end may be entirely worthy; but that, as we have been so long saying to ourselves and others, does not justify any means to its accomplishment. The wrong protested may be a thousand times more harmful than the wrong of illegal protest; is that justification enough? How should we decide, in practice, upon the rightness of certain methods—even methods deliberately disobedient and intrinsically unhappy—intended to further worthy social goals? This is one side, the practical side, of the puzzle.

As soon as we seek to resolve this practical question in any given case, we find ourselves facing a maze of difficult philosophical questions—questions with which we are all familiar, but that we had never before been forced to resolve in some conclusive way. This is the second, deeper aspect of the puzzle. Civil disobedience, its nature and justification, takes us directly to the core of some of the hardest and most important philosophical questions regarding social life. What are the limits of state authority? When, if ever, is a man justified in defying that authority, and on what grounds must such justification be based? What do we mean by the "rule of law" and how high in our catalogue of values must it remain? Nothing presses these questions upon us so quickly and so clearly as the practice of civil disobedience in a democracy, and the need to appraise it.

In this sphere Howard Zinn has written a most extraordinary book. I do not think his views entirely correct or even consistent; I find the frame within which they are put to be restrictive and disjointed; I am convinced that he is deeply mistaken on certain central issues. Yet the book is splendid—crisp and biting, reflective and insightful, sympathetic and humane. It deserves to be very widely read and very thoughtfully discussed.

The complexity of the issues with which this book deals renders it difficult to do it full justice briefly. It ranges over a great host of problems—the obligations of the citizen, the protection of the freedom of speech, the adequacy of our judicial and representative machinery, the need to devise new techniques of change—and there is hardly page on which the reader is not impelled to register strong objection, or further observation, or (most often) a cheer. Let me register here two strong objections, one observation and three cheers.

First, objections: The inadequacy of the standard "liberal" view of civil disobedience (of which Justice Fortas's pamphlet *Concerning Dissent and Civil Disobedience* is taken as the archetype) is

Zinn's principal target.

His attack takes the form of identifying a series of fundamental but (allegedly) mistaken propositions upon which the liberal view (more accurately, Fortas's view) is founded. These fallacies, as he calls them, in being widely and uncritically accepted, distort a realistic and healthy view both of the country itself and of civil disobedience as an instrument for change within it. Zinn argues that such disobedience offers rich possibilities for social reform, and ought to be more generously conceived and more liberally practiced. He is careful to say that civil disobedience is not all good, but he is sure that it most often is. Thus, he is obliged to deal with a number of the philosophical issues mentioned earlier, and at such critical points his argument is sometimes very weak.

The first great fallacy attacked is "that the rule of law has an intrinsic value apart from moral ends," where by "moral ends" Zinn means only real human needs. It is important for him that this be shown false, because so many (including Justice Fortas) have insisted that there is a universal duty to obey the law, and that this is a *moral* as well as a legal imperative. On the basis of this belief (Zinn argues), liberals mistakenly conclude that civil disobedience is always unjustifiable unless the law disobeyed is itself clearly and profoundly immoral.

Confusion develops quickly here. Zinn is quite right in maintaining that those who elevate the rule of law to an absolute, and who find every case of civil disobedience unjustifiable simply because it does break the law, and because breaking the law is always wrong, must suffer from serious moral blindness, and must have a cramped and distorted view of history and their own times. Obedience to law, and the order it promotes, is only one great value, after all, and must sometimes be measured against others with which it may come into conflict—economic justice, human liberty, international peace. To accomplish these, or others, the laws may be good instruments; but they may, on occasion, be obstacles instead. A rational citizen must make that judgment. In attacking those who are slavish in their submission to law, Zinn is wise and right.

He is not right or wise, however, when he concludes from this that, apart from the benefits achieved by specific good laws, there is no general moral obligation to obey the law. There is. It is a universal and, I submit, a very weighty obligation upon every citizen stemming from the universal human need to live in a society in which one can have reasonable expectations concerning the conduct (and the limitations upon the conduct) of one's fellow human beings. In that sense the rule of the law is both noble and practical, and it is a value of high moral import, quite apart from the particular content of individual laws. It is for this reason that one does have an obligation—a *moral* as well as a legal obligation—to obey a law even if he is quite convinced the law is bad. This, I think, is the force of the claim made by Fortas as well as the man in the street, that the laws always ought to be obeyed. However confusedly expressed, there is deep truth in the proposition that there is something *morally* wrong in breaking duly constituted laws. Indeed, Zinn exhibits a similar feeling himself when, later in the book, he expresses his distress at the willful disregard, on the part of the American government as a whole, for the rule of international law to which it is committed. He argues there that nations are bound by the same larger moral principles that bind individual men, and he is right. Among these is the principle that the laws ought to be obeyed.

Of course this principle cannot be absolutely compelling in every circumstance. The assumption that it is absolute, and the careless invocation of this principle whenever the disobedient protest in question happens to offend, are common errors against which Zinn might properly bridle. He goes much further than this, however, even to the extreme of rejecting the intrinsic moral value of government by law.

That is an unhappy turn. I have considerable confidence in Zinn's practical wisdom: but we are not governed by men such as he, nor are we likely to be. Individual judgments of what is right are often essential, but they are never sufficient for good human government. We must have laws, even if they are less good than they might be. In a healthy democratic community the laws will be respected and honored, although they are imperfect, because they are the laws. There is, therefore, a standing presumption against civil disobedience although that presumption may, in exceptional cases, be countered. This is what the standard liberal view is fumbling for; the cheap purposes to which the words of this principle are sometimes put do not in the least detract from its truth.

Of course our national community is, at present, far from healthy. The laws are often disregarded by officials sworn to obey them, and obeyed by citizens who have a higher obligation not to obey them. For it does not follow from the fact that there is a moral obligation to obey the law that such an obligation can never be overridden. It can. It is in such circumstances precisely that civil disobedience may prove justifiable or even obligatory. But what kinds of circumstances these might be, Zinn—partly because of the looseness of his argument—never finds it necessary to make clear.

The second fallacy under attack is that "the person who commits civil disobedience must accept his punishment as right." Zinn's argument comes to this: if the law is grossly unjust, any punishment for deliberately breaking it is unjust, and therefore the disobedient need not accept any such punishment administered by the state. Here again the position is weak, and the conclusion partly wrong, due to insufficient care and refinement in the analysis. The matter is complicated; Zinn tries to make it appear simple.

At an earlier point Zinn had introduced (less sharply than he might have) the distinction between what I have (elsewhere) called direct disobedience, in which the law broken is the very law protested, and indirect disobedience, in which the law broken is in some other way—symbolically or conventionally—relevant to the issue of the rightness of protest. What needs to be seen here is that this distinction is also importantly relevant to the issue of the rightness of punishment.

Normally, the civil disobedient does expect to be punished for his deliberately unlawful act. This is true because the disobedient is usually not a rebel (contrary to the suggestion of Zinn's language at some points) but a dedicated reformer within a larger system he is determined both to accept and to improve. Should he accept his punishment, then, as right? That depends on what he did, on what kind of law he broke. If he deliberately disobeyed a law he thought immoral in itself he is justified, of course, in fighting punishment in every reasonable way at his command, chiefly through the courts. He will seek to have the bad law struck down, or at least to have it declared inapplicable in his case. If he loses in the end, he is likely, as a citizen who is generally law-abiding, to accept the punishment, not as *right* but as a painful price he helps to pay for a law-governed community. If the law he broke really was in itself immoral (and we may be in some doubt about that), the legal system will have done an injustice; but we cannot allow every man to act as the judge in his own case. Of course justice is not always done, and the fight against bad laws must never stop, but miscarriages of justice do not, in themselves, justify the abandonment of a legal system.

If, on the other hand, the disobedient has deliberately broken what he knows to be itself a good law (a traffic or trespass law, or the like) to protest some other evil, say, the war in Vietnam, or oppression in the cities, it is right for him to be punished, not because he is a bad man but because punishment in such cases of indirect disobedience is a part—an essential part—of the act of protest itself. Indirect civil disobedience, if it is to be an effective tactic, must do more than disrupt; it must exhibit the depth and intensity of the commitment of the protester. To be a successful political act within the system, it must be a genuinely moral act within that system. It cannot be that, if the system is entirely disregarded. The beauty of this kind of protest lies in the fact that, though the law is broken, the system of laws is respected. Accepting the punishment, when one has deliberately broken a good law, is the only way to show that respect. To evade the punishment, therefore, is to emasculate the protest. The matter is more complex than Zinn's treatment of it would lead us to suppose.

Enough of criticism. One could raise similar objections to others among the arguments Zinn presents. But his work is so effective in opening our eyes and our minds that we profit more from considering his mistakes than from the muddy and superficial truths often encountered elsewhere.

Next, one observation: *Disobedience and Democracy* is a creative book, rich in insight and suggestion, but its positive impact is less than it could and should have been, largely because of the disjointed form in which it appears. That form is one of rebuttal; everything is framed as a response to Fortas's pamphlet (*Concerning Dissent and Civil Disobedience*) in which the several fallacies are alleged to appear.

But Fortas's work is itself poorly organized and loosely written, so that in providing a needed blow-by-blow response to it, Zinn is unhappily obliged to share some of its structural weakness. In fact, Zinn's nine fallacies are strung together with little in the way of unifying order; the consequence is that much of the constructive value of his argument is lost in the noise of battle. He has many important things to say about the need for imaginative techniques of social change and the forms they might take; but the force of what he says is partly obscured by the contest in which he is eager to score (and generally does) against a weaker opponent. In fairness it should be added that, treating these two small books as an intellectual confrontation, they present a highly absorbing spectacle, in which the Supreme Court Justice, a man of generous inclinations and considerable mental power, is bested again and again—shown to have been inconsistent, careless, occasionally shallow or unfair. A justice ought to write with greater depth and care than Fortas did, considering the gravity of the matter. Zinn is right in not going easy on him. But the upshot is, in both cases, that the threads which hang the whole together are thin and tangled.

Finally, three cheers, briefly put. One cheer for a short, punchy book, written in a prose that is plain and beautiful. Zinn writes with a directness and candor rare among scholarly men. Just reading the book is a pleasure.

A second cheer for Zinn as a perceptive critic of the American scene. He is a merciless enemy of hypocrisy and cruelty, and he makes us bite our collective lip. He is bitter, but not without hope. The largest thrust of his argument is that of a search for the instruments through which the radical reforms our condition demands can be effected with a minimum of violence and misery. He is good for us.

A third and final cheer for an author who comes through to his reader as a compassionate and gentle man, deeply anguished by the wrongs our nation does in his and all our names. Anguish cannot, by itself, justify civil disobedience as an instrument of change; but the compassion that underlies this book is desperately needed if the wrongs provoking disobedient protest are ever to be righted. ✳

THE PEOPLE? YES.

Bruce Kuklick, May 24, 1980

Review of **A People's History of the United States.** Bruce Kuklick is the Nichols Professor of American History Emeritus at the University of Pennsylvania.

Howard Zinn admits that "a people's history" is not the best description of his work, and I've tried to understand it by figuring out what would be the best description. The book is clearly about the oppression of the people: There are eloquent renditions of the destruction of Indian culture and rich analyses of the torment of the slaves, their revolts and their degradation after the Civil War. There are long explorations of the misery of the working class, its attempts to avoid becoming cannon fodder in American wars, and its struggles to form unions. Much time is also devoted to the study of left and radical politics. Finally, Zinn writes of the subjugation of women, although here I was struck by the brevity of his treatment, as if he were a relative latecomer to feminism who hadn't fully integrated its views into his own.

At the same time, Zinn has almost nothing to say about the daily texture of the social life of the people and, what is more surprising, there is no discussion of the people's religion—surely a central aspect of American experience in the seventeenth and eighteenth centuries and an important element in much of the nineteenth.

On its face, then, Zinn has written a book about class conflict and the awareness of such conflict among the masses. Eric Foner, writing for *The New York Times*, has pointed this out in arguing that Zinn has related only part of our history. What is needed, Foner says, is an integration of Zinn's narrative with a similar narrative about the elite. But Foner's analysis also falls short of understanding what Zinn is doing.

When Zinn comes to the post-1945 period, he actually spends much of his time exploring the doings of the elite. There is an extended summary of Cold War diplomacy from a "revisionist" standpoint and lengthy examinations of the connections among corporate, business and military leadership. Watergate is nothing if not an elite affair; yet Zinn has much to say about it.

The book is actually a radical textbook history of the United States. It's designed to give the left a usable past and, I think Zinn hopes, to inculcate into students a certain view of America. One gets a sense of this from the historical tempo. Zinn's 600 pages cover almost 500 years of history; yet one-third of the book is on the last sixty years, one-quarter on the last thirty. Fifteen percent of the book is spent on Zinn's favorite decade in the history of humankind—the 1960s.

I don't mean to derogate *A People's History* by assessing it as a radical textbook. Zinn writes clearly and articulately; his narrative is coherent and thematically unified. On the assumption that textbooks are socializing agents I prefer this sort of text to the usual ones celebrating industrialists and Presidents, texts for which Zinn has an ill-concealed but justifiable contempt.

At the same time, the book suffers the defects of the textbook genre. Its comprehension of issues is stunted; its understanding of materials is unnuanced. *A People's History* doesn't rise above these standard textbook problems in the way that, say, a rare sort of text like Carl Degler's *Out of Our Past* (1959) does. Degler's biases are liberal, but he brought to his task a subtlety and sophistication that Zinn doesn't possess.

Take Zinn's neglect of religion. Most of the time, I suspect, he believes it's the opiate of the masses, and wants to dismiss discussion of "the people" in their drugged state. But such a view not only ignores something important about the people but also overlooks the revolutionary and anti-elite dimension to American religious belief. The Massachusetts antinomian controversy, the

Salem witch trials, the periodic revivals and contemporary cult movements all display this potential, yet Zinn neglects them all.

Another set of examples: his radicalism to the contrary, Zinn is unable to realize that the resilience and shrewdness of American liberalism are the greatest enemies of the left reform he hopes for. He can't resist writing some sympathetic words about the New Deal, despite the fact that Franklin Roosevelt, more than any other single person, is responsible for the twentieth-century success of the system Zinn abhors. When he treats Joe McCarthy, he goes no further than the liberal notion that the Wisconsin Senator was a grotesque anti-Communist. Zinn doesn't see that McCarthy saw through a glass darkly: part of his message to "the people" was that internationalist diplomacy was the product of a smug ruling class whose policies had the chief consequence of sending the ruled off to needless wars. This veiled message was also surely part of McCarthy's appeal.

Perhaps the most significant example comes from reviewing Zinn's attempts to grasp the failures of "the people" over five centuries. His story is of continuous expressions of class consciousness and solidarity. For Zinn, the workers, the poor, the oppressed know who their enemies are, and their history is one of persistent and recurring attempts to throw off the oppressors' yoke. Yet they never succeed; indeed, Zinn effectively admits that they've failed again and again by noting how successful "the system" has been at containing or transforming protest. How do we explain the people's constant failure and the elite's constant success?

Zinn's text is so blunted that it has only mechanistic answers to this question. The ruling group found "a wonderfully useful device," the symbols of nationhood; "the profit system" began to look overseas; the system had "an instinctual response" for survival; "American capitalism" needed international rivalry and demanded a national consensus for war, and "the system" always responded to pressures by "finding new forms of control."

I don't find these explanations very sensitive; they reflect, again, the failures of the textbook genre. But all this is not to say that Zinn's is not an excellent text. It's rather to say that one should read Carl Degler first. ✳

HE SHALL NOT BE MOVED

Paul Buhle, November 21, 1994

Review of **You Can't Be Neutral on a Moving Train: A Personal History of Our Times.**
Paul Buhle is a prolific author and editor of works on the history of the American left. In 2008 he collaborated with Howard Zinn and the cartoonist Mike Konopacki on a graphic **People's History of American Empire.**

I have always imagined that historian Howard Zinn somehow took part in the multitudinous radical movements of the 1840s-50s, campaigning for abolition, women's rights, dress reform[8] and nonviolence. A rare Jew among Yankees and African-Americans, he would have commanded the platform with figures like Susan B. Anthony and Frederick Douglass, held his own against hostile audiences and broadcast the prospects for universal freedom. Something about Zinn's style and bearing suggests the prophetic profile so com-

---

8.   Dress reform was a Victorian-era movement to make clothing, especially women's undergarments, more practical and less restrictive.

mon to radicals in those days and so rare in our own.

Actually, Zinn grew up in a blue-collar Brooklyn family in the 1920s and '30s, son of a waiter named Eddie and a hard-pressed immigrant mother from Irkutsk, Siberia. At the ripe age of 10, Howard bought a cheap set of Dickens with newspaper coupons, and came to understand poverty in new ways. Almost accidentally he found himself at an antifascist demonstration in Times Square, like Charlie Chaplin in *Modern Times* picking up a red flag and seeing thousands fall into step behind him. In real life, New York's finest rushed the demonstrators, leaving Zinn with a blurred memory and a lump on the head.

This was Zinn's introduction to the left, along with reading Upton Sinclair, Marx and Engels. He got a job in the Brooklyn Navy Yard and then joined the Army Air Corps at 20, in 1943. Eager to bomb the fascists, he flew missions across Germany, Hungary and Czechoslovakia. Educated by a Trotskyist gunner who described the war as an imperialist adventure (Zinn had already read Arthur Koestler's novel of disillusionment with Stalinism, *The Yogi and the Commissar*), he was pained to realize that he and his colleagues had destroyed the French city of Royan along with the German forces holed up there. This marked the beginning of a deep disillusionment with war.

Mustered out and already married to a political soulmate, Zinn went to NYU and then Columbia on the GI Bill. Meanwhile his family grew, and he worked nights in a warehouse, joining District

65 of the old Retail, Wholesale and Department Store workers. After he hurt his back he took up adjunct college teaching, determinedly winding up his PhD. From here on, the story ceases to be mainly personal: Zinn started work at all-black Spelman College in 1956.

He was just looking for a job, but he found the crusade that he had, perhaps, been preparing himself for. Atlanta was the right place to be, even if few effects of *Brown v. Board of Education* or the Montgomery bus boycott could yet be seen. Zinn soon took his students and a few others from Morehouse College to visit the Georgia state legislature, where they attempted to sit in the whites-only section, stirring a near-riot. (One of the students from Morehouse was Julian Bond.) By 1959, the faculty adviser of the campus Social Science Club, Zinn found himself prompting the desegregation of the Carnegie Library in Atlanta, as his students asked politely for copies of the Declaration of Independence or the Constitution. They won their point. Then came the escalating rounds of sit-ins, jail, appeals, boycotts and still more demonstrations. Almost always Zinn was on hand, offering an apartment for meetings as well as his kindly encouragement and strategic acumen. He modestly takes no credit except for being there. In a book blurb, Marian Wright Edelman (originally Marian Wright, a student of Zinn's at Spelman) describes her teacher as totally inspirational, a formidable influence on the movement spreading around him.

Zinn plunged into the national spotlight when he took an assignment for the Southern Regional Council reporting on the anti-segregation struggle in Albany, Georgia. Zinn's report, condemning the unwillingness of the Kennedy Justice Department to assist the victims, hit the front page of *The New York Times*. *The Nation* soon published Zinn's moving essay "Kennedy: The Reluctant Emancipator" (December 1, 1962).

Now SNCC jumped into the act in Albany, with Zinn as one of its two adult advisers (the other was civil rights veteran Ella Baker). Stokely Carmichael, Bob Zellner and Charles Sherrod, along with Bernice Johnson (Reagon) of the Albany SNCC Freedom Singers and later, Sweet Honey in the Rock (Zinn helped her get into Spelman College)—the most spectacular circle of activists since the industrial union movement of the 1930s—soon had a big story to tell.

Zinn decided to tell it, in the book titled *SNCC: The New Abolitionists* (1964). He had earlier proved himself an able scholar with his prizewinning *LaGuardia in Congress* (1959); now he turned to his real métier, the popular narrative. Hardly a better current history has been written than this instant classic, which combined oral history with a novelistic narrative and a burning sincerity. Zinn had made his mark as an unusual type of scholar, redefining American radicalism while explaining the emergence of a radical generation younger than himself. He says at the end of *SNCC* that their language and lives "give only a hint of what it is about SNCC that worries traditional liberalism." The young activists hinted at socialist egalitarianism, "but to put it this way freezes what is really a fluid attitude, directed at ending deprivation and equalizing wealth, but completely open about ways to do this," a radicalism of mood more than of doctrinal certainty.

One can fairly complain that Zinn did not see the downside to this prospect. Tossed on the seas of youthful expectancy and indifferent to solid organization, SNCC and the rest of the New Left were prone to the ravages of short-term disappointment as much as to the tricks of security agencies and the rhetoric of future neoliberals. But one cannot doubt the poignancy of Zinn's later reflections: "How awful they were, those days in the South, in the movement, and how they were the greatest days of our lives."

Zinn paid an unexpected price, dismissal from Spelman (Alice Walker, another of his students, left in protest). He headed north, to then-liberal Boston University, in 1964. And once again he placed himself in a political cockpit. By April 1965, Zinn was speaking at the first of the anti–Vietnam War rallies on the Boston Common, sharing a platform with Herbert Marcuse. As a veteran both of the Second World War and the civil rights struggle, Zinn had credibility, a ringing voice and a wonderfully straightforward manner. He projected that public self along with a skillful analysis in a little book, *Vietnam: The Logic of Withdrawal*, which sold well at demonstrations and went through eight quick editions. A Cleveland *Plain Dealer* columnist suggested that the final chapter of Zinn's book, written as a model presidential address, would make a real President giving it "one of the great men of history." Johnson and his would-be successor,

Hubert Humphrey, lacked the courage to try it.

The deepening disappointment in American liberal leaders marks a deep-textual frustration inevitable in *You Can't Be Neutral*. Zinn offsets the mood with other hopeful and even funny moments, like FBI agents, in hot pursuit of Father Daniel Berrigan, rushing the stage at a 1970 Passover peace ceremony. (The lights immediately went out, and by the time they came on again Berrigan had vanished into a Bread and Puppet Theatre creation.) But the book does not move toward a happy ending. Zinn's popular narrative, *A People's History of the United States* (1980), indeed, became the standard textbook alternative against the reality of Reagan America.

The new Boston University president (and clown prince of neoconservatism), John Silber, ached to cashier the much-admired radical professor who drew hundreds of enthusiastic students each semester. "The more democratic a university is, the lousier it is," said Silber, delicately explaining his educational philosophy a few years later in *The New York Times*. But Zinn already had tenure. And happily for the rest of us, Silber could not convince Massachusetts voters to launch his gubernatorial career from the little corporate kingdom he had created on campus.

Zinn closes his volume with an epilogue, "The Possibility of Hope," in which he insists that "small acts, when multiplied by millions of people, can transform the world." True, no doubt, although the thought seems rather too pious at a moment in which we require a drastic shift of the radical paradigm just to keep up with the multiple human and environmental calamities ahead. We probably need a science-fiction version of Zinn just now, half prophet and half cyberpunk.

Still, he has a point about our underestimation of the trouble we cause our rulers. The sudden and unexpected appearance of social movements at various moments of the past certainly makes elites nervous, when they think of history at all. Meanwhile, a new, sleek-faced brand of writers, from the conservative think tank to the bestseller shelf to PBS documentaries, is indeed hard at work trying to bury that past in hyperbole about free markets and American innocence.

If *You Can't Be Neutral on a Moving Train* seems sometimes less than Zinn's best, it is because he has too much modesty to construct a world view out of his own experiences. However, he is a good read, as always. And the casual or intense Zinn-watcher will surely be touched by his urging to "live *now* as we think human beings should live, in defiance of all that is bad around us." These homely phrases remind us of the simple, often disguised promise that remains alive in human decency and in a willingness to learn from history. ✳

SOME TRUTHS ARE NOT SELF-EVIDENT

RED FOX? THE UNLIKELY UNION OF MURDOCH AND ZINN

Tom Gogola, April 5, 1999

Tom Gogola is a veteran journalist who in 2011 won the Sidney Hillman Foundation's Sidney Award for an article in **New York** magazine on counter-productive regulations in the commercial fishing industry.

T he contracts are signed, the treatment is being written and Fox Television plans to fast-track production on a ten-to-twelve-hour miniseries based on lefty historian Howard Zinn's *A People's History of the United States*, scheduled to run early next year. With celebrity muscle provided in amply hunky doses by Zinn allies and series co-producers Ben Affleck and Matt Damon, Fox is banking on Page Six sex appeal to sell Zinn's sobering tales to the tabloid masses.

Skeptical media watchers have been clucking about this project since Rupert Murdoch's minions first started negotiating with Zinn and company last spring. After many months of wrangling, all parties recently agreed on a six-part dramatization of key sections of Zinn's book, based around the individual exploits of average Americans caught up in major historical moments.

This unlikely venture finds its genesis in a scene from Damon and Affleck's 1997 breakthrough film, *Good Will Hunting*, in which Damon praises Zinn's book. As it turned out, the Zinn and Damon families were old friends from Newton, Massachusetts. ("I went to his high school play," says Zinn.) A producer at Fox, Marci Pool, who had read and enjoyed the award-winning book in college, got her bosses' OK to negotiate to buy the TV rights, which previously had been held by Globalvision executive producer Danny Schechter. After a couple of marathon sessions in Los Angeles, attended by Zinn, Affleck, Damon, *Good Will* producer Chris Moore (the "Gang Of Four," as Zinn calls them) and Fox Television Studios brass, a contract was hammered out late last year. Zinn says he was adamant that the final product adhere to the "class, race and antiwar consciousness" of the book, and the contract contains language to the effect that "the series will be true to the point of view of the book," says Zinn.

The studio ponied up $50 million for the series, and the Gang of Four quickly hired screenwriter Jeremy Pikser (who's up for an Oscar for his work on the Fox-produced *Bulworth*) to produce a treatment. When that's completed, it goes to Fox for approval. Bob Dylan and Winona Ryder have already signed on—he's singing, she's acting—and John Cusack and Danny Glover are negotiating for roles. "That's a huge help," says Pool. "To get that level of interest from talent is very unusual and very difficult in television."

At the time of this writing, the contours of the treatment are taking shape. Zinn reports that some of the storylines being contemplated are a dramatization of the resistance movement in the abolitionist period, as seen through the eyes of a slave, and a section devoted to a deserter (or, at the very least, a dissenter) from the American Revolution. According to screenwriter Jeremy Pikser, "You can't dramatize a textbook, and you can't fake a docudrama as a drama, so I've invented a whole life story for a dockworker in the Revolution, and his great-granddaughter turns up later as a Lowell millworker. It's just about the most exciting project I've ever worked on."

Taken individually, these are interesting subjects with populist appeal and built-in gravitas that goes deeper than the surface-skating entertainment generally offered up on the Hitler, er, History Channel. But Zinn is acutely aware that in presenting historical moments as seen through the eyes of just plain folks, he runs the risk of losing the populist forest for the trees. "That's been a worry from the beginning, and we're going to work to overcome that, and find a way to make connections and larger points that put the individual episodes into broader contexts."

You'd think Fox would rather those links not be made. After all, the archconservative Rupert Murdoch isn't going to sell Zinn the rope the amiable socialist professor would hang him with. Even though Zinn says he hopes his final product "doesn't pass Murdoch's political litmus test," some wonder whether even Matt Damon's pearly whites will be enough to save *A People's History* if it strays too far to the left.

"That's not the right question, frankly," says Pool. "Putting a miniseries on the air is a business, and the bottom line is that this is a good project for the network. The book is history as told by people who didn't win the battles or the wars, and that is something that Fox audiences can identify with. Our audience is young, and they identify with struggle. No one inside the company has said anything to me about the politics—not that they won't at some point, but I don't see why they would." As Zinn observes, "To simply do another history is not going to excite a lot of viewers, and the fact that there's a controversial set of messages is precisely what might attract a large audience, which is really what Fox cares about." But, as Pikser points out, "As Fox has made clear, our audience is not the PBS audience. We've got to make it play. It has to be an entertaining, interesting story that you'll want to watch."

It also must be said that Murdoch has shown some restraint in meddling with his network. He did drop the BBC World Service from his Star TV in China a few years back, claiming it posed a potential threat to his Asian business interests; more recently, he canceled a biopic on Anita Hill because it strayed too far to the "We Believe Anita" side of things. But as Fox sponsors Zinn's critical look at the unseemly corners of American history, it is also looking ahead to the next epoch with *Futurama*, the year-3,000 Matt Groening cartoon series that debuted in March. With unapologetic doses of *Simpsons*-style archcynicism, the series typifies the profitable niche Fox has carved for itself. It remains the "little-guy network," airing programs that are by turns scrappy, hip, craven, pointlessly violent and willfully lowbrow. Everyone loves an underdog, and Fox plays its youthful, rebellious status like a fiddle.

In that sense *A People's History* is a perfect fit for Fox: Murdoch is to Zinn what Pat Buchanan is to Jerry Brown—the flip side of the same populist coin. And "coin" is what it's all about. ✳

Murdoch's Fox eventually put the kibosh on the Zinn mini-series project.

ZINN'S CRITICAL HISTORY

Eric Foner, February 22, 2010

Eric Foner is DeWitt Clinton Professor of
History at Columbia University and a member
of **The Nation**'s editorial board.

F riedrich Nietzsche once identified three approaches to the
writing of history: the monumental, the antiquarian and the
critical, the last being history "that judges and condemns."
Howard Zinn, who died on January 27 at 87, wrote the third
kind. Unlike many historians, he was not afraid to speak out about
the difference between right and wrong.

Zinn was best known, of course, as the author of *A People's
History of the United States*, which since its publication in 1980 has
introduced millions of readers to his vision of the American past.
Few historians manage to reach a broad nonacademic audience.
Those who do generally write Nietzsche's monumental history,

works that celebrate great men (the Founding Fathers, Abraham Lincoln) or heroic events (the building of the Transcontinental Railroad, World War II). Zinn's history was different. Through *A People's History* and various spinoffs (including a recent dramatization by prominent actors of a collection of documents on the History Channel), Zinn's public learned about ordinary Americans' struggles for justice, equality and power.

I have long been struck by how many excellent students of history first had their passion for the past sparked by reading Howard Zinn. Sometimes, to be sure, his account tended toward the Manichaean, an oversimplified narrative of the battle between the forces of light and darkness. But *A People's History* taught an inspiring and salutary lesson—that despite all too frequent repression, if America has a history to celebrate it lies in the social movements that have made this a better country. As for past heroes, Zinn insisted, one should look not to presidents or captains of industry but to radicals such as Frederick Douglass, Susan B. Anthony and Eugene V. Debs.

Before writing *A People's History*, Zinn published *SNCC: The New Abolitionists* (1964). This book grew out of his experience teaching at Spelman College, an institution for young black women in Atlanta, and his participation in the civil rights movement. It remains essential reading for anyone seeking to understand the upheavals of the '60s. Its subtitle is worth noting. At a time when most historians still depicted nineteenth-century abolitionists as neurotic misfits whose agitation brought on an unnecessary war, Zinn identified their campaign against slavery as the beginning of a long, unfinished struggle for racial justice.

A veteran of World War II, Zinn spoke frequently about the horrors of war, lending his voice to those opposed to American involvement in Vietnam and, more recently, Iraq and Afghanistan. He was a passionate critic of the national security system and the militarization of American life.

A few years ago, I lectured at St. Olaf College in Northfield, Minnesota (the hometown of the late, lamented Senator Paul Wellstone). Zinn had been there a few days before, and across the top of the student newspaper was emblazoned the headline Zinn Attacks State. I sent Howard a copy. We laughingly agreed that he could not have a more appropriate epitaph. ✳

ACKNOWLEDGMENTS

Thanks to Douglas Layman, the Wayne, New Jersey, high school history teacher who introduced me to A People's History, *and to Judith Long, whose three and half decades of service to* The Nation *now draw to a close. Credit as well belongs to Omar Rubio for his elegant design, to Mel Grey and to Art Stupar, and to every person who has ever passed to someone else a book by Howard Zinn.* —Richard Kreitner